MW00928702

Pony Tales

To Mary,
Finally face to face,
good Luck with the
horses!
Happy Birthday!!
Chuck & Marion
Hakotomshi

Pony Tales

Captivating Stories About
Thoroughbred Horse Racing

Chuck and Marion Sokolowski

Copyright © 2016 by Chuck and Marion Sokolowski.

Library of Congress Control Number: 2016916631
ISBN: Hardcover   978-1-5245-4811-7
                Softcover   978-1-5245-4810-0
                eBook   978-1-5245-4809-4

All rights reserved. No part of this book may be reproduced or transmitted in any form or by any means, electronic or mechanical, including photocopying, recording, or by any information storage and retrieval system, without permission in writing from the copyright owner.

Any people depicted in stock imagery provided by Thinkstock are models, and such images are being used for illustrative purposes only.
Certain stock imagery © Thinkstock.

Print information available on the last page.

Rev. date: 11/08/2016

To order additional copies of this book, contact:
Xlibris
1-888-795-4274
www.Xlibris.com
Orders@Xlibris.com
748990

For direct orders of this book, contact:
www.ourponytales.com

CONTENTS

**A Collection of Stories from America's
Favorite Racetracks**

Preface

Visualize in your mind's eye a map that will negotiate your travels through an incredible and colorful maze of tales, twisting and turning at every corner and street, grassy meadow, and countryside, engulfing you with every yarn. This passage flows from my mind to the hand clutching the pen so you may enter my world as you read.

The road map that guides you will start in upstate New York in a small, sleepy hamlet named Saratoga Springs. Envision yourself at that venue in the humid midday sun in 1863, when President Lincoln occupied the White House, the Civil War was raging, and the outrageous, witty, and adored William R. Travers, along with Cornelius Vanderbilt and others, opened the famous Thoroughbred racetrack nicknamed the Spa. Considered to be the oldest racetrack in America—and since I had been weaned there—you will be reading many a tale born of this venue. Funny they may be, I may be putting you on the bit, very Runyonesque like.

So please sit back and enjoy your tour through this majestic world of equine tales.

It Had to Be Done

After the long, cold, icy, snowy, never-ending day after day of winter, it is now one week before the vernal equinox—March Madness—beginning of the baseball season and the buildup to the 2015 Triple Crown races. That is why "it had to be done." So go ahead and ask the silly question: what had to be done? It's a simple answer. I've begun to get my butt in gear and start to seriously put this manuscript together in an attempt to complete it by the time this Thoroughbred racing season gets underway. In my humble opinion, the Thoroughbred season begins with the Triple Crown events, the Saratoga meeting, and culminates with the Breeders' Cup events. My wife says, "Same old, same old." I say, "Au contraire." Yes, the teams are the same, the players will be the same, and the horses will always be the horses—but each player, game, and horse will inevitably show you something a lot different than they did before, creating an entirely different outcome. To an avid sports fan, it is the sole epitome and reason you return again and again for more and more.

With all this being said, my wife and I just returned from a three-week vacation from Arizona and California. There were two reasons: one, to get into the warm and sunny weather, and secondly, to collaborate somewhat with an old friend after an eighteen-year absence. The stories you are about to read in this journey will mainly capture and tell you of a period of time in the last half century or so involving myself; my wife, Marion; my friend Jim, and his wife, Lucy.

My wife, Marion, and Jim's wife, Lucy, prior to this statement, have somehow unwittingly been sort of duped into this rivalry between Jim and me beginning sometime in 1955. How it started, I don't know;

however, it very quickly blossomed from subtle to voracious. In a heartbeat, we could be funny, engaging, or bitter enemies all at the same time, all over some silly, unimportant matter. In an attempt to try to separate fact from fiction, we sat down for a few hours over lunch, reminiscing and trying to accomplish how to elaborate on this story. Understand he has an engaging, charismatic nature when speaking to you. He's convincing, Svengali-like, that you did something that you actually did not do, or remember something that you or he did not say. This is truly a gift.

At this meeting, I gave him a number of the first few original short stories in an attempt to find out his opinion, since he said in a previous phone conversation that he would give me an honest and true evaluation, pulling no punches. Believe it or not, I believe him. I subsequently asked what he thought, and I received a positive reaction. With that, I am forging ahead, albeit they will be to the best of my recollection.

Far to Go

It was Thursday, May 13, 1943, when my friend James Gerard burst upon the scene, and his father, Jack, proclaimed with his hands in the air, "King James," since he was the first male child born in the family since the early part of the century. World War II was on, Hitler was marching through Europe, and rationing was enforced in the United States. The United States was drawn into World War II on December 8, 1941, after the attack on Pearl Harbor on December 7, 1941. On June 6, 1944, the United States was trying to conclude the defeat of the Nazis with the invasion of Normandy. James Gerard, almost fourteen months of age, started to get his legs under him. And little known to him, I was about to enter the world, strangely enough, approximately a month later on a Thursday, July 13, 1944. Some ten years went by, neither of us knowing of the other's existence when, apparently, the inevitable happened. In September, just after Labor Day of that year, we both crossed paths playing softball on the ball field of the school we attended, he as a sixth grader and I as a fifth grader. But then we went our separate ways, he moving on to junior high school and I remaining for one more year in grade school.

A few years went by before we rekindled our friendship since that all-important one-year period when we went our separate ways, being involved with different circles of friends. At the end of high school, our friendship blossomed, and other than short periods of time in our relationship, it has gone on for over half a century.

As it turned out, the relationship was enhanced by the fact that we had many things in common, not just the ironic fact of both being born (although a year apart) on Thursdays and the thirteenth day of the month. Some may say that the number 13 is not necessarily all that lucky; but apparently, it has kept our friendship together for many years.

Jack—that is Broadway Jack—James Gerard's (or Jimmy's) father, brought his family up to Saratoga for the month of August back in the late fifties and early sixties to summer on Saratoga Lake. Coincidentally, it also happened to be the racing season at the Spa. Jack was drawn to the ponies like a moth to fire. He was certainly one who could knock off not two but several birds with one stone. So now you get the picture. It was at this group of cottages on Palmers Maple Shade that Jack and his family vacationed every year with friends, track goers, trainers, and jockeys, and Jimmy and I first learned how to read the *Tele*, learned about the sport, all the blue bloods, racing history, and handicap the races of the day.

Jack was able to spend this kind of time during the summers vacationing since he was a fire inspector for FDNY. He had somewhat of an auspicious clientele that he visited on a regular basis to inspect their facilities. On his watch were such notables as Ebbets Field, Aqueduct Racetrack, Jamaica Racetrack, and a number of other sporting venues and the occasional sugar plant and more mundane businesses. Once I remember going to visit Jimmy at his beachside cottage in Breezy Point, and Jack was standing there in his bathrobe and slippers at about one thirty in the afternoon with the New York Mets baseball game on TV. He apparently became a Mets fan after the Dodgers left town, heading for the West Coast. At that time, Jimmy appeared from a back room, and as we got noisy, Jack told us to shut up. He was making a phone call to cover his butt, and if anyone called, he had just left or hadn't arrived to do the inspection and return a call to him. And then he promptly sat down and started watching the game again.

He didn't get the moniker Broadway Jack for nothing. Jack's past, let's say, was slightly tarnished. He had some whimsical quotes and a few harebrained schemes, some of which worked. A few come to mind, such as answering a print ad saying, "For $1.99, we will send you a solid 100 percent copper engraving of President Abraham Lincoln." When you answered the ad and bought this beautiful piece of art, you received in the mail a shiny new uncirculated penny. The other one I remember was that for $4.99, you would receive a half dozen of twelve-by-eighteen-inch, 100 percent cotton towels; within a period of a few days, you would get your handi-wipes. He had some little idiosyncrasies that I remember well. When we were in our late teens and Jimmy would ask to borrow some money to go out for the evening or he wanted something, he would always ask, "Dad, can I do this?" or "Can I have that?" One day, Jimmy said, "Dad, can I borrow twenty dollars?"

His father said, "Sure you can, but you may not."

Then I remember well, this being said at a neighborhood bar, Jimmy came back to his stool at the other end and told me this. I looked over, and his father was motioning me with his finger to come over. And when I walked over, he pulled out a wad from his pocket and asked me, "How much you want to borrow?"

I said nothing. He said, "Are you sure? Anything, whatever you want."

When I repeated no, he said, "I got it. If you borrow money from me, Jimmy will borrow it from you. I know I'll get it back from you, but you won't get it back from him." That was Broadway Jack.

Broadway Jack

In the spring of '55, six months after the Cleveland Indians beat the New York Giants four straight to win the World Series of 1954, four months before my eleventh birthday and as baseball season started, we were all eager to start playing ball in preparation for the end of the school year field day. My fifth-grade class along with the sixth-grade class went out to the playground and baseball field, choosing up sides for a softball game. The sixth graders had a new kid on the team, and they put him in right field; that's where you buried the worst player so he couldn't hurt your team. We didn't know his name and just watched him as the game developed.

Early in the game, a ball was hit out to short right center field. Out of nowhere comes this new kid with an incredible diving one-hand catch, rolls over dirty and dusty, and jumps to his feet, holding the ball over his head for the last out of the inning. We soon found out his name was Jim Dundon. He robbed me of an extra base hit. From that point on, we became good friends. He could play the field, hit, and he sure as hell could run. This was the type of guy I wanted to be associated with. He had a sharp tongue and could always back it up. We seemed to go together like ham and eggs.

The following year, he went on to junior high school while I was finishing my last year in grammar school. The year after that, my first year in junior high school, we seemed to be hanging out again. He had a propensity for gambling. It was always "I'll bet you this" and "I'll bet you that" even at that age.

By 1957, we were known as a couple of hustlers. By the time we were fourteen and fifteen, the 1958 Kentucky Derby was approaching.

Calumet Farm entered Tim Tam, who was considered a heavy favorite for the Kentucky Derby. Tim Tam did not run to expectations, and a long shot by the name of Iron Leige won the Kentucky Derby that year.

Jimmy and I became interested in horse racing at that age. Jim's father, Jack Dundon, a fire inspector for the City of New York, worked out of an engine company in the Wyckoff Street area of Brooklyn. He was always looking at the *Morning Telegraph* (commonly called the *Tele*), the precursor to today's *Daily Racing Form*. He was always known to his good friends as Broadway Jack. Someone yelled over, "Hey, Broadway, where are you going today?"

He replied, "Aqueduct."

The voice shouted back, "Anything good running?"

"Yeah, the four horse in the third race."

You see, everyone knew that Jack rubbed elbows with a lot of the biggies at the track—jockeys, trainers, or owners—while "inspecting" for the fire department. Ha! Jimmy and I always kept a keen ear to what Jack had to say, always trying to put some scratch in our pockets. And we learned very quickly of the art of handicapping and soon began going to the races in hopes of profit, fame, and fortune.

A few weeks later, Jimmy and I got up the intestinal fortitude (commonly known as guts) to sneak into Aqueduct Racetrack. We scrounged up six dollars, left home, and made it into the track. We had never put a bet in at the racetrack, and it took us some time to attempt that. We were worried that we'd get caught and be thrown in jail; we didn't know what to expect since we were underage. I don't know if we were more worried about getting caught or successfully placing a bet. After what seemed to be an hour of "no you do it, uh-uh, no you do it," Jimmy, being older, finally went to the two-dollar win window and put two dollars on a horse called Daring Heart and found it amazingly easy to get away with it. Strutting back like a big man, we went down to the rail to watch the race. As amazing as it sounds, Daring Heart came thundering home and won easily, paying $214.20. We went crazy! At that age, it was like hitting the lottery. Suddenly, Jimmy felt the clasp of someone's hand on the back of his neck. I looked up and said, "Shiiii—t!" I was looking at Jimmy with his father behind him Grabbing his neck, Jack opened his mouth and said, "What are you doing here?"

Jimmy gave him every lame excuse, but Jack didn't buy it. He grabbed the ticket out of Jimmy's hand and looked at it, noting it was a winning ticket and a big payoff. He shoved it in his pocket, released Jimmy, and kicked him in the butt, saying, "Get the hell out of here. You're supposed to be in school."

Jimmy turned, saying, "But, Dad."

Jack, smiling, tilted his head to the right and said, "Whaaat?" Then he turned and walked away, saying, "Get your ass home."

Apparently, he cashed the ticket, and it was the last we ever saw of that money.

Understanding how easy it must have been, we were hooked. A couple of weeks later, we found ourselves back again. We both thought this game must be easy. Jimmy made a bet or two, and his horses lost. I only had a few dollars in my pocket, waited a couple of races, then looked at a horse by the name of Blackbeard—a dark, almost black, handsome bay ridden by Braulio Baeza. The horse looked good on the racetrack, and I was intent on placing a bet to win on this horse. Jimmy, the expert handicapper he was at that time, tried to talk me out of the bet, saying the horse didn't have a chance. I placed the bet anyway. The gates opened, two or three horses jumped to the lead, and Baeza took a hold of Blackbeard in next to last position, ten or eleven lengths from the lead. As they turned into the far turn, Baeza started to make his patented come-from-behind move past horses in the stretch, and in an exciting finish, he got up to win by a head. My first winner. Jimmy said, "Yeah, mine paid $200. What did yours pay?"

"Eighteen sixty," I said. Yeah, but then I showed him two tickets totaling $37.20.

He smiled and said "all right!" and slapped my hand. And at least we kept the money this time since Jack wasn't around.

At the end of the day, we took the bus back to Valley Stream and still had twenty-five dollars—half a week's salary. We went to the Valley Stream Diner and ordered hamburgers, fries, and Cokes like big spenders. We congratulated ourselves on having a great day and started talking about future exploits.

Handicapping the day's races!

Wiseguys

The fifties were coming to an end. Jimmy and I were in our latter teen years in 1960, and we started taking to the track every Saturday, knowing it all and digging deep into the *Tele*, the predecessor to today's *Daily Racing Form*. At fifty cents a pop, it was a luxury that we could ill afford since we were barely making a dollar an hour working during the week, but could certainly not afford to go without, buying and sharing one along with one program.

We were smart enough to weave our way through the crowds, avoiding the touts hawking their daily picks. What I recall was always rushing to get there and stupidly making the double without having enough time to spend on handicapping not only one race but two. Obviously, you get it—we rarely won early in the day. Once we had the opportunity to go beyond the first two races and handicap properly, we stood a better chance at winning. Quite different in those early days when there were no exotic bets other than the daily double—no exactas, quinellas, trifectas, superfectas, pick six, and other such wagering. So, obviously, it was much easier to pick one horse to win, place, or show— that is to say to finish first, second, or third. It was always our way or the highway. That was us. Early on, we would catch winners and make some money often enough; but occasionally, we could not understand why we would lose certain races. Though knuckleheads we were at that time, we still realized that the addition of blinkers would more than likely be a positive in the change of the horse's equipment. So, naturally, we also thought unknowingly that an aluminum pad or a bar shoe was also a positive. It didn't take us too long to differentiate changes of equipment, and surprisingly, we started winning more often. You see, blinkers would enhance a horse's natural speed and keep his mind on racing and would eliminate seeing a horse coming up alongside, challenging their lead and subsequently emboldening the horse into getting to the finish line first. On the contrary, an aluminum pad or a bar shoe would be added to the horse's equipment in an effort to dull the sensitivity of tender hooves and allowing them to race more confidently. So in effect, any horse with the addition of an aluminum pad or bar shoe may have durability problems—which, in effect, is a negative and should be considered as such in handicapping.

Soon after that, we recognized that we had a winning combination if we would handicap individually. Now we would make our selections, rating them 1, 2, and 3. Then comparing our selections and assigning in reverse order three points for the number 1 selection, two points for number 2, and one point for number 3, we would analyze and compare both his and mine and come up with winners more often than not when selections came up similarly. Most races were ordinary, and we both made similar competitive numbers; and a winner was usually obvious, so it was easy to make that choice. On occasion, none of our top three would be alike in any way, shape, or form. We would then have to carry on a conversation in depth why this was so and usually would pass on the race or throw in a two-dollar flyer on one of the long shots.

On a rare occasion—and I will give you an example—Jimmy would pick the no. 6 horse on top; the no.1, second; and the no. 10, third. And I would pick the no. 4 horse on top; the no. 6 horse, second; and the no. 7 horse, third. Comparing these choices if the no. 6 horse's odds were 17-1, the no. 1 horse was 2-1, and the no. 10 horse, 5-1, and my first choice, the no. 4 horse, was 4-1, and the no. 6 was 17-1, and the no. 8 was 5-1, we would have a discussion and start putting the pros and cons together concerning the no. 6 horse. The discussion would center around why we both rated him so highly, and more often than not, we would come up with the rare but lucrative winner of the race, paying $37.60 to win. Somewhere along the way, that apparently wasn't good enough, and the old cliché "my way or the highway" set in.

Not knowing how it started or when it started, we began making arguments about the pros and cons of certain horses and somehow challenged each other in an attempt to beat each other, rather than constructively handicapping for the greater good and winning races. I guess at that point, it was more important to beat each other rather than to win races. Obviously, we soon got over that, and things began to normalize again.

In the sixties until the seventies, Jimmy and I set a tradition of going up to Saratoga at least once a year. Speaking of it today in remembering those early years, we would look at each other and say, "I can't believe we would drive up at 5:00 a.m., two hundred miles just for the day, talking horses, drinking coffee from Long Island to Saratoga, arriving there, having breakfast at Ann's, going to the track all day, leaving and having a drink at Pennell's, Siro's, or Reds, and driving back in the evening." We would usually go up on a Saturday, as that's when the stakes races were run, in hopes to see the likes of a *Kelso, Roman Brother, Gun Bow, Beau Purple, or Dr. Fager* run. On the third Saturday of May, Preakness day 1969, I found myself and Jim wearing tuxedos on his wedding day, watching *Majestic Prince* on TV, trained by Johnny Longden and ridden by Bill Hartack, beating *Arts and Letters* to the wire and becoming the only undefeated three-year-old to ever have an attempt to capture the Triple Crown three weeks later in the running of the Belmont Stakes. Unfortunately, the day *Braulio Baeza* finished second in the Preakness turned the tables and defeated the great son of *Hill Rise*. The following year, Jimmy and I reversed positions, and I got married in October, finishing off the 1960s with a new era upon us.

King James

It seemed like we'd always find a way to create havoc and trouble for ourselves dealing with Broadway Jack. In our early twenties, a few years later, Jimmy and I went to Saratoga for a few days during the racing season once again in hopes of making it big. Knowing that his father was staying in a cabin at the lake with some of his buddies, we thought we'd pay him a visit. We found him in the usual cabin near Frank Martin's cabin on the lake with a number of his cronies. He asked us if we wanted to join him for breakfast and what the hell we were doing there. We told him we came up for a few days to play the ponies and were staying at the Thoroughbred Motel. We asked him if he wanted to go to the track with us. He said he was going to take it easy and had some business of his own but asked if we would mind running in the doubles for him. We told him "sure." He handed Jimmy twenty dollars and wrote down his daily doubles.

Mistake number 1. We went to the track, got there an hour or so before the first race, and started doing some handicapping. As post time approached, Jimmy and I went to the windows and put in our daily doubles. When the race was over, our horses lost, and a twenty-six-dollar horse won the race. Kicking ourselves, we realized the horse that won was a horse we were looking at but decided not to play. As a handicapper, sometimes you look back to see exactly what might have caused you to eliminate the horse and not bet him. As we turned the page back in the racing form, we both realized that we hadn't put in Broadway Jack's daily doubles. Jimmy pulled out the sheet of paper with the twenty dollars and Jack's bets, and sure as hell, there it was. His top pick in the first race was the horse that won. We were dead, and we were going to be crucified. Those were the first thoughts that ran through our minds. I said, "Wait a minute, Jimmy, we're not dead yet. Remember, he could lose the second race, and he'll be out of the double anyway." In other words, we could sit back. And if it didn't win, we would have no explaining to do, and he would have simply lost his twenty bucks. Or we could fess up.

Jimmy said, "No way, there's got to be a better solution." We could either tell him we got there too late or we lost the money, and everything would be fine. Of course, the best thing that could happen was his daily double wouldn't win, and we could walk away with the twenty in our pockets and no one would be the wiser. Of course, his horse did win, and we were screwed—like always.

After the following race, along came a smiling Broadway Jack, and he yelled out to Jimmy from forty or fifty feet away. "Hey, I been looking for ya. The double paid $213 and change." He was looking for his money. We decided we had to fess up. He caught us unaware by showing up at the track. When we told him that we forgot to put the bet in, he looked at us and gave us a blank stare, and we thought we were in deep shit. He shook his head and looked down at us, back and forth. I have no idea how many times, and he said, "I should have known better. Look at you two, you and my son, King James. King James," he said with a smirk on his face.

Jack proceeded to tell me the story about King James, looking at both of us. After eight consecutive girls born into the family, finally a boy was born. So long in anticipation of a male, Jimmy was dubbed and heralded as "King James," the first boy born to the family. Jack couldn't resist. For the rest of the afternoon, he constantly needled Jimmy as he held a beer time and again in his right hand and extended his left hand, palm upward, in Jimmy's direction, saying "King James, my son, King James" as if in a Shakespearean manner. That was all he could say for the rest of the afternoon until he got tired of it.

He located his buddies, and as Jack approached them, he wandered from us. He shook his head left and right with his hands in the air, saying, "I should have known better. I should have known better. Never again, never again. King James, King James."

A Horse of a Different Color

In my opinion, I strongly believe I should set the tempo, the stage, and establish the setting that brings me to the subject matter of this book. Many years ago, early on as a youngster, I had an affinity for animals and history. I quickly narrowed the subject matter to Thoroughbred racehorses, the excitement of racing, and the early history of the United States.

My first thoughts go back to the late fifties—Tim Tam and Calumet Farms and remembering his loss as a three-year-old in the Kentucky Derby of 1958. After that, at the age of fourteen, came some exciting periods, usually during the spring season and Triple Crown events through the sixties. At that point, I learned about American history, the Revolution, the Civil War, and even earlier than that, the exploits of Christopher Columbus. I simply remember more about President Lincoln, the Emancipation Proclamation, the fighting between North and South, and the birth of contentious racing of Thoroughbreds in our country.

A new era of the sixties came about. The first presidential election was televised, for all intents and purposes, between Kennedy and Nixon and their debates.

The winner of that Derby of 1961 was owned by Katherine Price, trained by Jack Price, her husband, and bred by a little-known sire named Saggy—who, if you don't recall, stood with a monumental breeding fee of $5,000. Considering that sum, I thought anything was possible in the sport of kings. During that decade, in 1962, the Kentucky Derby was won by Decidedly, and his record time of just over two minutes and one second stood for a decade. Then came '63, won by

Braulio Baeza aboard Chateaugay, the upset undefeated winner of that year. You said undefeated upset winner. That's right! You see, that year, there were a number of undefeated horses in the fray. The first of which was Candy Spots, owned and trained by Rex Ellsworth, with strange black and white spots on the hind quarters, thus the name Candy Spots. Next, a Thoroughbred named No Robbery. The story of this horse was that Greentree Stables owners had a habit of naming horses after famous quotes. When naming a Thoroughbred, you must submit, in ranking order, five names. The reason is, if a name has already been selected in the past twenty-five years, it cannot be used again. So they decided to name their horse Fair Exchange with, I believe, number 2, No Robbery.

When the Jockey Club did their due diligence with the submission of these names from Greentree Stables, they found a horse with the name Fair Exchange registered, thus No Robbery was chosen for the English proverb, "A fair exchange is no robbery."

Number 3 was Captain Harry F. Guggenheim, owner of Cain Hoy Stables' Never Bend. All three were looking for favoritism in the Derby as favorites ran second, third, and fifth beaten by Chateaugay. The long shot of the four unbeaten colts, somewhat forgotten in the mix going off at 8–1, paying eighteen dollars in change to win to everybody's surprise. Newscasters of the day said "Unbeaten colt wins the Kentucky Derby, but not any of the ones you think."

In 1964, another truly great Thoroughbred came along and subsequently became (possibly) the greatest turf sire of all time, and without any doubt, the greatest Canadian-bred of all time from Windfield Farm—Northern Dancer. In that year, he won the Kentucky Derby, went on to win the Preakness, and was considered a virtual Triple Crown winner (a first since 1948), only to be upset by Quadrangle in the Belmont Stakes. During the decade of the sixties, great talent—both equine and human—took to the tracks of America. Just to enlighten those who were not there, I can give you a blow-by-blow account of the great happenings of the day.

Bill Hartack rider of the great Northern Dancer, his fourth winning mount in a career that ended up with another one later in the decade by the name of Majestic Prince, who won the 1969 version of the race and, at that time, went on to win not only the Kentucky Derby but also the Preakness. By the way, Majestic Prince in 1969 was attempting to establish the milestone of being the only undefeated Triple Crown winner in history. That day, a lesser-known colt by the name of Arts and Letters, trained by Mack Miller and owned by Paul Mellon, thwarted his chance to become the only undefeated Triple Crown winner ever. During the sixties, there were outstanding horses—such as Damascus, Buckpasser, and Dr. Fager—that I really thought I had seen the best of the best.

Au contraire, believe it or not, along comes the dawning of the 1970s. In my humble opinion, the best decade ever.

In those days, the seventies, I heard tell from some of the old-timers about the likes of Man o' War, Count Fleet, Citation, Assault, Phar Lap, War Admiral, and Seabiscuit among others from the turn of the century and before. At that time, the old-timers would argue, most of them vehemently, that the horses of the first half of the century would unequivocally beat anything today—virtually any track, any distance, and any surface. I believed then in the '70s, and now at the turn of the millennium, that the '70s were unparalleled.

I wasn't there in the first half of the twentieth century from 1900 to 1950, so I will have to consider many different aspects of the game. And from what I heard over the years in many different venues of racing and what I have actually seen, I have come to these conclusions. In 1970, the year my girlfriend and I married, little did I know, a foal was born on March 30 of that year, by Bold Ruler out of the mare Somethingroyal at Meadow Stable in Virginia, owned by Christopher T. Chenery. This weanling was also being handled by Penny Tweedy, his daughter, and subsequently became two-year-old champion of 1972. He was unwittingly dubbed Big Red when most people argued the fact that Big Red was the nickname of Man O' War from a different era. Little did they know, like a premonition, a second coming was about to unfold. The reason I claim that this big chestnut, along with one other that I will mention later, tops the list of all-time greats is that if you really look closely, you can almost see the Pegasus-like wings. Secretariat, for one reason and one reason only, tops that list for the fact that during that period, he went on to establish stakes records in all three events, culminating in a thirty-one-length victory in the Belmont Stakes in track record time with the second-place finisher, Sham, also breaking the track record. That in itself is a crowning achievement. In 1973, after winning the Derby and the Preakness, crowds were wondering if there would ever be a Triple Crown winner in their lifetime; after all, it was some twenty-five years between drinks. Now in the spring of 2015, my argument is that those records have not only held for forty-one years (maybe there's a possibility of another Triple Crown winner), but a purist would say "Did he equal or better Secretariat's record times in all three?" They say records are made to be broken, but these will last forever. So we have Big Red.

My horse of another color was a strapping 16.2 hands, dark bay or brown, but I could swear to you in 1974, her glistening dappled coat sure looked black to me as David Whitely saddled and gave a leg up to Vince Bracciale on this most spectacular two-year-old daughter of Reviewer, owned by Stuart S. Janey—Ruffian. Undefeated in all her races, her running style tracking from off the pace, she would soon get the lead; and once that happened, she would come home in a widening stride and pull away under a hand ride. She and Secretariat are the only horses I've ever seen that would run with that conviction. On July 6, 1975, she was entered in a match race against Foolish Pleasure at Belmont Park, both champion three-year-olds. I believe many called it the battle of the sexes, colt vs. filly, in a day and age when tennis champions and adversaries Bobby Riggs and Billie Jean King would be pitted against each other. It just seemed to be the order of the day. On that fateful Sunday, I can remember the two loading in the gate, Ruffian on the inside, Foolish Pleasure on the outside. After both breaking alertly, noses apart in the first furlong, as they lengthened stride and picked up speed going the first quarter, Ruffian started to pull away by almost a half-length. With a sudden bobble in her stride, Foolish Pleasure went by her, Jacinto Vasquez desperately trying to pull the filly up. She had broken down, shattering her sesamoids in her right foreleg near the ankle. Vasquez, finally bringing her to a stop, jumped off; and a couple of days later, she had to be put down. Since she had never lost after taking a lead, I can only make the outrageous assumption that she would have undoubtedly pulled away and won that race if the tragedy hadn't occurred. But for the fact that we will never know, if in fact, should Secretariat have been bred to Ruffian, what would the possibilities be? Since there's Bold Ruler blood in both Secretariat and Ruffian!

As the decade went on, another colt appeared, although at first glance not nearly as regally bred or handsome as the other two mentioned, and incredibly less expensive in the sales ring at a mere sixteen thousand or so, but fast as all hell. Seattle Slew, at second glance, actually was a grandson of the great Bold Ruler. So now you get the drift. In 1977, Billy Turner and Jean Cruget captured the second Triple Crown of the decade. The following year, Louis Wolfson, the owner of Harbor View Farms, his trainer Laz Barrera, and apprentice youngster Stevie Cauthen pulled off one of the greatest feats of Thoroughbred racing by narrowly defeating John Velasquez and Calumet's indomitable Alydar to win the third Triple Crown of the decade as Affirmed held the lead in each race and dug down deep, never allowing Alydar to take the lead. In each event, it appeared the second-place finisher, Alydar, could go on by and beat this California colt at will, but never did.

The first Saturday in May of '79 came, and an incredible athlete named Spectacular Bid sauntered onto the track in front of the grandstand, trained by Buddy Delp and ridden by Ronnie Franklin. Could it be three Triple Crowns in a row? He easily put away his rivals and drew off to win the Kentucky Derby and again in the Preakness, only to come home a struggling third three weeks later in the Belmont. Earlier that week, the horse stepped on a safety pin, but it was removed. Swelling and slight infection occurred, but he still ran on race day.

Not only great horses such as Secretariat, Ruffian, Seattle Slew, Affirmed, Alydar, and Spectacular Bid exhibited their courage on the racetrack, but another slightly lesser-known steed appeared as well. Originally first ridden by Heliodoro Gustines and then the more well-known Willie "The Shoe" Shoemaker, Forego ran fourth in the 1973 Kentucky Derby to Secretariat and went on to a glorious career, carrying more weight (130/140 lb.) many a time. Forego was owned by Mrs. Martha F. Gerry of Lazy F Ranch. Any arguments about the best decade of them all, anyone?

Just about all my adult life, from a teenager at the age of fourteen through the end of the twentieth century, and now at the dawning of the new millennium, and seeing that a few intriguing movies have since come to life on the big screen along with over fifty years involved in the sport, I decided to challenge myself with this publication. With my background, knowledge, and affinity for the sport, I attempt to capture a period of time in the sport along with a smattering of US history and personal experiences that are humorous, factual, and intriguing to enlighten and encourage the general public to come into my fascinating world of the equine athlete for your pleasure.

Prince Valiant and Friar Chuck

It was the spring of 1971. Jimmy and I were in our late twenties. Jimmy married first to a gal named Lucy in the spring of 1969, and I second to Marion in the fall of 1970. In those days, we were both half-assed, floundering around, working at menial nondescript jobs, and not earning a hell of a lot of cash. I had a brilliant idea. Since Marion and I had just come back from a vacation in South Florida in January, I had engaged in conversation with her cousins in Hollywood, Florida. The conversation concerned some real estate that was for sale—a steal and also a one-acre property that Marion and I had purchased near what is now known as Disney World. I subsequently engaged Jimmy, who worked with Pan Am Airlines at the time, and knowing that he was able to fly at super inexpensive employee rates, he was fast becoming a jet-setter. Since we were inseparable since the age of ten or eleven in the mid-fifties, I thought we might become partners in this venture. With this as a motive to incorporate him along the way, and also since he constantly reminded me of his ability to fly virtually anywhere in the world for only a few bucks, I asked him if there was any way he could snooker a couple of tickets to fly to Florida. He made some kind of trade-off with a coworker, and since in those days there were virtually no security problems, he consummated the deal and we paid only the tax on the flight, next to nothing. We were going to check out the real estate. Along with that, we heard about openings with the Miami Police Department and the security of a good job, and since Jimmy's father was now living in the Clearwater/Tampa Bay area, we were going to look him up while we were there.

Off into the wild blue yonder to Miami at 4 to 5:00 a.m. on a Friday, and we would soon be landing at about 8:00 a.m. Tired and weary and in for a long weekend, we were off to pick up our rental car. We were in town to check out a strip mall in Hollywood and also a property that Marion and I had purchased earlier the previous year in Kissimmee/Orlando. Deciding that we should look good for our police interview at Miami police headquarters, we said, "Let's see if we can get a shave and haircut so we look decent." Oddly enough, we saw a barbershop on our way to Miami; we stopped and tried to get in, but the door was locked. As we approached, an elderly gentleman in a smock motioned us to come in. He put his hands to his head then put his hand in his pocket, pulled out a key, unlocked the door, and we were in; thank God. He asked, "What can I do for you?" And I told him, "We just got off a flight from New York and we could use a shave and a haircut." You have to understand that Jimmy had what they call in the day a Prince Valiant doo, that is virtually with his curly, dirty brown Irish hair long over his ears, down his neck, and almost page boyish, and me with my wavy doo-wop DA also halfway down the ears, we were a sight to behold. He quickly wrapped us in steaming hot towels, and we both immediately conked out. It seemed like fifteen minutes later when he said OK, clapped his hands, and said, "Guys, you're done." He handed Jimmy a mirror and I heard a blood-curdling scream.

I yelled out "What's the matter?" He handed me the mirror and said, "Go ahead, take a look." After I bounced around the floors and walls a few times and screamed at the barber—although elderly, probably in his midfifties, ha ha—he opened his arms and said quizzically, "What's wrong? You don't like the haircuts?" Jimmy and I looked at each other, handed him the highly inflated dollar and a half, absolutely no tip, shook our heads, and left. I guess we never actually instructed him that what we wanted was a trim, not a buzz cut. The last time I'd had a buzz cut was when I was in the army. We rushed to one of the hotels on the Miami strip, entered the men's room, quickly changed to suits and ties, and went to our interviews at police headquarters. We took the necessary tests, answered all the questions, went before a doctor and a panel of three. They accepted Jimmy but put a nix on me. Obviously, I asked the question, "How come?" They said, "You're five feet seven and three-fourth inches in height, your friend here is five-ten. The standard for acceptance to the academy other than passing muster, you must be a minimum of five-eight." Just my luck. If I didn't have bad luck, I'd have no luck at all.

Since Jimmy had not been to Florida and I had at least the one time, I knew the ropes. It was fast approaching noontime and I asked him about a few races at Gulfstream. He nodded and we were off to play the double at Gulfstream. Since we hadn't checked into a hotel at that point, we stopped at another hotel along the way, made a quick change into our civvies, and proceeded to lose a few dollars at Gulfstream. Jimmy said Gulfstream was beautiful. I told him, "If you want to see something really nice, Hialeah makes this look like a dump." Marion and I had been to Hialeah earlier in the winter, the bougainvillea which were in bloom, the lake, and the flamingos were absolutely breathtaking. We left Gulfstream after the third race. Strange, because we were diehards, we wouldn't be leaving any sooner than they crossed the finish line after the ninth race. Back in the day, unlike today, a card meant nine races and only nine. You could virtually set your watch by race time. Being hungry, we found a small shack on the interstate accidentally, since we had turned south trying to catch the I-95 north. As we zipped by Captain Bill's like radar, my eyes caught a handwritten sign above the shack that said All U Can Eat Shrimp $1.99 in large print, in smaller print, and Fish. That was right up our alley. We quickly made a U-turn and went in, checked out their menu, and decided to go for the gusto. We ordered a platter for each of us and a bottle of beer each. When the food came, it looked absolutely great. Since we had lost at the track, it was a no-brainer that we were going to save at the dining table. So quickly, as we sipped the ice-cold brews straight out of the bottles, Jimmy said to me, "Hold on, put your beer down. I've got this angle. Look at the food." Understand this—Jimmy grew up in the fast food business; he had read the menu, and the fish, chips, and the shrimp were all beer battered and deep fried. He quickly said, "Go easy on the beer. They deep fry the food with a little bit of yeast. If you drink too much, the yeast will bloat you and you won't be able to eat that much." We proceeded to finish two humungous platters of shrimp and the fish, strips of the abundant and inexpensive red snapper. The waiter came back and said, "How was it guys? Can I bring you another beer?" "No, we're good, but why don't you bring us another platter of fish and chips. It was excellent." After an hour and a half, we slugged down the last of our now warm beer, left a dollar tip, picked up the bill, and paid at the register. Believe it or not, the gourmet meal, $1.99 times $2.35 cents a beer, and the tax was covered with a fin.

Bellies full and totally satisfied, we were off. It was getting a little late. It was a little after two as we headed north to visit Jimmy's father, Broadway Jack, mentioned in a few other stories. He was north across on the Gulf Coast in the Tampa/Clearwater area. On the way, we had to make a pit stop and check out the property which was near Orlando, "the future site of Disney World." Being light out till about seven midday on Friday, there was virtually no traffic on the I-95. We were having a great day. Jim was driving. He started moving at about 75/80 mph. I said to him, "It's a 55 mph zone. Back in the day, everything was 55." The road was a two-lane concrete highway in each direction separated by a two-hundred-foot grassy median. Sure as hell all that did was invite Jimmy to step it up to 85 or 90. Problem was, highway patrol used radar guns in those days. Since the highway was totally empty, for reasons I don't know, Jimmy stepped it up, saying, "I wonder if this piece of crap car can actually hit 120 on the speedometer." I said, "Take it easy. You're crazy."

As luck had it coming, in the opposite direction, I saw a smokie. As we flashed past him, I saw his lights go on. I said, "Jimmy, he's crossing over. He's after us." Instead of slowing down, Jimmy checked out the speedometer, he hit 105, 110 hits the 120, and said, "I guess it does top out." Since we were going so fast, we left the smokie in the dust. By the time he regained any momentum coming after us, we were two to three miles past him pulling away, only trouble it was pretty straight and flat. I was praying for some little turn in the road, some undulation in the road, and I said to Jimmy, "As soon as we get out of his view, look for an exit and we're gone." As I'm speaking, we catch a break at a little dip in the road, and a slight bend to the right up flashes an exit two miles, and fortunately out of view of the gendarme. Doing well over 100, we took a sweeping turn, had to be about at 50, 60 mph, maybe more, virtually on two wheels. Pulling aside a grapefruit grove, we got out, stretched our legs, plucked off two nice ruby reds, and stopped off to pick up a cake at a local general store. Jimmy looked at me and said, "I think we're almost at the four freeway, which goes through Orlando to Clearwater and Tampa." Surprisingly, it was four thirty; we had some daylight left.

By the time we reached Orlando, we started to get somewhat tired and we realized we hadn't slept, had a lousy day, and that we better start thinking about getting a room. Rooms were at a premium at that hour, but we finally got a Motel 6. They only had one room with two doubles. I think we actually paid the price of the logo, $6.66. I'm not absolutely sure of that, but push comes to shove, I'd make book on it. Showered and relaxed, give or take, a few hours later, we decided let's go and grab some dinner. Much to our surprise, most places were starting to close for the evening. We looked at each other when one proprietor said, "What do you think, this is New York." But he said there was a little piano bar about a mile down the road. He gave us the name, which I don't recall right now. So for the rest of the evening, we sat at the piano bar and actually had some pub fare. It was absolutely outstanding with good live music, that along with scotch after scotch. We asked the singer his name and exchanged pleasantries as he said, "Bruce." He knocked out a lot of doo-wop. During the evening, all three of us were getting sloshed, and we nicknamed him. We were yelling out his handle "Go Go Loose Bruce" as we got the whole crowd having quite an evening. Leaving after last call at three or four in the morning, we looked at each other and said, "What the hell did we get a room for?"

We promptly went back to get a few hours of shut-eye. Waking up about 9:00 a.m. on Saturday morning, we trudged on with quite an agenda next on the itinerary. Bleary-eyed, we went on to check out the property at Kissimmee. Finally, about a half hour later getting there, we were directed into this big, open, swampy area, and lo and behold, into a clearing pops up this beautiful state-of-the-art hunting lodge with just a handful of cars. We got out and entered. We were welcomed, we sat down with a young lady, and she asked if we wanted to tour the property. Answering yes, she said, "You do know you have to go out on horseback." We said, "Fine, right up our alley," and she directed us to the stable area. Another young lady in her twenties saddled up three horses and promptly took us out along this trail.

After about ten minutes, we found ourselves deep in the brush, when all of a sudden, the horses came to a halt and a wild boar ambled off. It had to be well over a hundred pounds, big tusks and all, a razorback. As we went a little farther, we saw an area that looked like it was just plowed by a farmer because the earth was turned up. We asked the gal what it was and she said, "Did you see that boar? That's what they do out here, looking for root vegetables. That's why we're out here on horseback since they sense the horses, not humans." A few hundred yards from that area, she pointed out the property and said, "This is as far as we can go." We asked why, and she replied, "Your property is somewhere out there. It's all marsh right now, waiting to be developed in the next few years."

Jimmy looked at me and he said, "You bought swampland." I don't remember the company we bought it from, but I do remember the history of the company involved in selling land. The principal behind the company was Charles Antell, developer of hair products for both men and women. His most famous product was Formula no. 9 hair pomade product, advertised back in the days of black-and-white TV.

Next on the agenda—on to Broadway Jack—was a total bust. Jimmy thought he would surprise him and show up unannounced. Turned out, he couldn't find hide nor hair of him. So truthfully, with that futile effort, we headed back to Gulfstream and got there late in the day, played the last two races, once again losing, and checked in at the Spanish Villa, a small hotel in Ft. Lauderdale, the same place where my wife and I had stayed in January. I called Jerry to see the strip mall, and he said unfortunately, the guy rescinded the sale of the property. So now zero for two. I said to Jimmy, "After we have something to eat, let's take a ride to the greyhound track." We got there about eight in the evening for the first race, picked up programs, and I said to Jimmy, "Give me twenty-five dollars." He said, "What do you want twenty-five dollars for?" And I said, "I'll put twenty-five dollars. We'll start with fifty dollars and partner up." He said "yeah, whatever" and ponied up.

Jimmy then said, "This is ridiculous. How the hell do you handicap this?"

I said, "Trust me. Marion and I were here in January and I made beaucoup bucks." (It was a relative number in those days.) As the dogs loaded into their starting box, the mechanical rabbit started to move on the rail, and the caller said, "Here comes the bunny," meaning the rabbit and the doors flip open, and these crazy dogs were on the hunt. The track was crowded. It was a Saturday night. Jimmy couldn't even see over the heads and shoulders of the crowd and neither could I. In less than thirty seconds, the race was over, dogs clustered around the mechanical rabbit, the handlers took the dogs back to the kennels, and the crowd dispersed.

Jimmy said, "That's it, let's go." I said what, and he said, "I don't bet my money on anything I can't see and is over in less than half a minute."

It was hard to reason with him. The deal I struck was, "Let's do it this way. I only lost ten of the fifty. How about leaving after one more race, and if we lose, we go. If we win, we stay and we go after we lose another race." He said, "OK, but don't ask me for any more money." Realizing I had to ration the dough, I decided to put a limit and a plan together. Four dollars to win, two-dollar exacta box, and a two-dollar quinella, equaling ten dollars, and I could find a way to stay for a few more races. Handicapping the greyhounds to me personally was easy. I was like a duck taking to water. We left after the tenth race, winning eight consecutive races either running first or second and collecting on quite a few winning tickets, never varying from my ten dollar bet, the standard for that evening. We walked away with over $450 between us. We headed back and got a good night's sleep at the hotel.

Since it was spring, the weather was really nice and our flight wasn't until late in the afternoon. We went to the batting cages down the road and hit a few balls and raised a few eyebrows as a couple of people gathered around as the balls were pinging off our bats. One guy yelled out, "What team do you play for?" Almost in unison, I said Tigers and Jimmy said Indians. The guy said, "What's your names?" And putting them on, we told them a couple of obscure names. In response, the guy said, "Never heard of you." We looked at each other and said, "Spring training rookies." The guy said, "You look a little old for rookies." We shrugged, said, "Oh well," and walked away. Our only regret? No one asked us for autographs, them or the kids, but putting these locals on was a gas. We went to the airport, turned in the car, got on our flight, and returned to Kennedy Airport in New York, happy to be home with a little extra jingle in our pockets.

Ambiance of Saratoga

Nestled in the foothills of the Adirondacks, Saratoga is located midway between Albany and Lake George, New York. This quaint little hamlet is two hundred miles north and five hours by car from Long Island. Going north, taking the New York State Thruway to Exit 25, Route 9, and exiting, you continue north past Albany, crossing the Mohawk River made famous in the early days of movies by *Drums Along the Mohawk*. It seems nothing has changed in this "countryfied" area except blacktopped highways and the simple bridge crossing. Looking down at the river from the bridge, you could almost expect to see the Iroquois paddling down the river in a birchbark canoe—either being hunted by the French (a formidable foe) or approaching one of their own villages during the time of the Revolutionary War. Traveling farther for sixty minutes or so, we reach Saratoga. This was in the early '60s, as President Eisenhower's interstate construction program had not been completed yet. Today, you would simply go to the next exit and take the Northway up past Albany, all superhighway to Saratoga.

Two miles from the highway, the village of Saratoga appears, loaded with charm and history. Saratoga's streets are lined by turn-of-the-century porched homes reflecting early Americana. Set back on huge parcels of rolling lawns, you may come upon one of which has been turned into a bed-and-breakfast, another an antique shop, and some of those set upon larger parcels, close to the racetrack, will be converted to parking lots accommodating the overflow of automobiles prior to race time in the month of August.

There are number of local graveyards in and about town with headstones dating back two hundred years, showing scars and weathered by time since the Battle of Saratoga and the Revolutionary War. This town of one hundred and fifty thousand grows to over half a million during the racing season in the month of August. During the racing season, the streets are filled with passersby, vacationers, and racing enthusiasts stopping to peer in the shops, restaurants, and hotels. Walking down Main Street, you cannot help but notice an elegant small old hotel. On the second floor overlooking the street, the veranda made of black filigreed wrought iron reminds you for an instant of those in New Orleans. In the late 1800s, this establishment served as a gambler's haven. If you let your mind wander a moment, you could envision rock'em, sock'em moments when a pistol-packing card player might have pulled out a derringer, accusing another of cheating at cards. There was legalized gambling in this town.

Entering town from the southeast, you approach the famous mineral baths of the Roaring Twenties and the exclusive Gideon Putnam Hotel, often frequented by the Whitneys, the Vanderbilts, the Mellons, and the like as the charm abounds. Don't be surprised on any given August day to accidentally bump into a celebrity walking the streets of Saratoga.

Feeling hungry? You just might want to stop for breakfast at Ann's, an old diner-type restaurant. You can't miss it with its twenty-foot white-and-red rooster peering at you from off the country road—impeccably clean, unbelievably priced, the food to die for. Entering the establishment, we always picked up our racing form and greeted the old man in his seventies, having known him for many years (but, ironically, not well enough to know his name).

Or should you want to be tantalized with a morning buffet at the aforementioned hotel with the history of gambling, you could sit leisurely outside at a table on the street just under the overhang of the porch, handicap the day's races, watch the passersby, and absorb the wonderful morning.

Now, if you require a little excitement and hubbub, you would definitely not pass up Mother's for breakfast. On a narrow side street, on a slight downhill location away from the crowd, the real horse crowd gathers for breakfast at this quaint haunt on Philadelphia Street. Hearty breakfasts were the norm, with homemade muffins and pastries alongside three eggs, sausage, bacon, and terrific home fries, all for a pittance. Tips on the upcoming races was the order of the day. Most of the crowd were stable hands, exercise riders, trainers, jockeys, and jockey agents. On one given morning, two brash youngsters—the dynamic duo of jockey Chris Antley and his agent, Drew Mollica—appeared at the arch of the doorway, as if to say "OK, guys, we're here" in a brazen tone, and seated themselves. No one thought—after Stevie Cauthen, rider for the Triple Crown winner Affirmed—that another young jock could take his place in the spotlight so quickly. Anything Antley was riding was a good bet, due mainly to his agent's innate ability to handicap a race, his charisma to charm a trainer, acquire the mount, and to fulfill the riding assignment with win after win after win. Any wager on an Antley-ridden horse from six furlongs to a mile and a half was like the best thing since sliced bread. You could bet Antley and just wait there on line and cash a winning ticket. We couldn't attest; although there might have been some nice restaurants for lunch, we would always eat trackside.

After a day's racing, dining at Lillian's in town, the Trade Winds with its piano bar, or Siro's on the backstretch might be a thought. Before leaving town and after dinner, the lounge at the Inn at Saratoga was beckoning us for a nightcap. The food was excellent, the ambiance perfect. But one of our favorite haunts was Joe Collins, a restaurant with down-to-earth prices and festive foods (Italian, steaks, fish) and a rather large menu. It was always too good to pass up. You had to get there early; otherwise, there was a long wait. When you were seated, everyone was talking about the day at the races. Along would come a teenager with hot-off-the-presses pink sheets still drying from the printer—a small ten-page periodical of the day's results of each race, along with photos of the finish and tomorrow's entries. We could probably handicap the daily double for the following day before the food was served, and the wives would say, "Haven't you had enough? Why don't you put down the papers and enjoy dinner." Or to be more adventurous, you might want to travel farther north near the border of Vermont to Rutland, where you'd come upon Wally's and have an incredible full-pound medium-rare prime rib with all the trimmings at a respectable $9.95. Of course, you would have an ulterior motive to catch the evening's Thoroughbred races at Green Mountain Racetrack in the Berkshires just over the border in Vermont, a sixty-minute ride from Saratoga. Returning late to catch some shut-eye back in Saratoga, anticipating an early start for the following day's racing.

Travelling Union Avenue from town, approaching the gates to Saratoga racetrack, the oldest Thoroughbred racetrack in America, you wind through the parking areas on a narrow one-lane blacktop road with attendants in white Banlon shirts with the red insignia of Saratoga directing you off to the side on the dirt and grassy areas in between the elms to a parking spot. You can enter the grandstand area or the clubhouse. At 7:00 a.m., after the early-morning mist has risen to meet the warm sun, you would be seated at a table covered with a red-and-white gingham tablecloth with the typical condiments and a bud vase sporting a single geranium. Ordering breakfast and coffee, you could watch a number of the most famous trainers—such as D. Wayne Lukas, John Russell, Ross Fenstermaker, and Sheryl Ward—leading their precocious Thoroughbreds (owned by Eugene Klein, Ogden Phipps, Fred W. Hooper, and other famous owners) onto the track for a morning workout, preparing for an upcoming race at Saratoga.

Strolling through the clubhouse area, you realize you're walking on old hardwood plank floors, integrated in some areas with concrete. The pillars of wood, reaching up to a wooden roof accommodating the spires, have been there since the track was opened. Moving into the grandstand area on the main level, you realize that this entire facility has been standing since the turn of the century in its original wooden splendor. Walking away from the clubhouse and grandstand area, entering the grounds, you notice a building indicating Racing Officials and Stewards Only, and another building saying Jockeys Only. This is where the valets prepare the jockey's colors and equipment, readying them for the jockey's upcoming race. These outbuildings, all of wood, are painted white with green trim. Approximately fifteen or twenty minutes prior to the race, jockeys dressed in their silks, caps, and riding boots, whip and goggles in hand, emerge from their locker rooms to walk amongst the crowd while curious people and children ask for autographs. They carry on conversations, making their way toward the horses being saddled under the enormous elms in what is considered a random outdoor paddock area. The bugler calls RIDERS UP. Owners, trainers, and jockeys surrounding the horses give final racing instructions to the jockey and give him a leg up, moving in single file to approach the entrance to the racing oval. And within ten minutes, the first race of the day, and for the last hundred years or more, the first half of the daily double will be run.

In one area stands a large white gazebo with the words *Saratoga Springs* appearing in red. Within its structure appears a concrete fountain painted white and somewhat rusted. This rust is caused by the high ferrous and mineral content of the water. People flock to this area with bottles and cups being handed out as they approach to have a drink of the famous Saratoga Springs water; they seem to enjoy it, kind of relish it, and bring some back to their picnic table area. This water is now bottled in a clear bottle with the name *Saratoga* printed sideways and sells at a hefty price in local markets nationally. Quite frankly, in my opinion, it is bitter and nasty.

This being Tuesday (a dark day, meaning no racing), we took in the sights and went to check in at the Thoroughbred Motel, a favorite place of ours. The Thoroughbred Motel is located on the outskirts of town, no more than a mile and a half from the track itself. You had to keep an eye out. If not, you could easily pass it up since the motel and cabins were off to the right and down a small hill in a semicircular area, and you could barely see the top of the cabins. Once again, we were greeted by Bill, the proprietor, and his wife. They invited us over to the pool area, where they usually have coffee and donuts for their guests throughout the morning and early afternoon. The coffee was up, and the donuts were out.

We joined others already handicapping the following day's races, and along comes Angelo and Bill, saying, "You're back for more punishment this year." After spending a while catching up, since we hadn't seen them since last racing season, Jimmy and I went to the office with Bill and paid our bill in advance, to make sure that we didn't gamble away at least that part of it. We always stayed in adjoining cabins. Bill gave us the keys to cabins 21 and 22. These cabins were single-room attached cabins, sharing a bath with a large screened-in front porch. There were fourteen separate standing two-cabin units. We opened our cabins, unpacked, cleaned up, dressed for the evening, and went to Joe Collins for dinner. Exhausted after a two-hundred-mile trip, we went to bed that night with high expectations of tomorrow's racing.

Marion & Chuck, Jim & Lucy 1971 Saratoga

Chuck & Jim August 2016 Talking horses 45 years later at Saratoga

7777777

Seven sevens—one might consider that lucky. Maybe not. Thinking about it now and reflecting back, it was either 1972 or 1973 for sure, matters not, but the gist of this story brings me back. The four of us—my friend Jimmy and his wife, Lucy, and Marion and myself—set out that Tuesday, let's say August 3. There was no racing that day with Tuesday's being dark. We were up at Saratoga as married couples and begrudgingly making sure to come up with a dark day in mind so as to give the girls a break from racing. We arrived at the Thoroughbred Motel early morning. With morning starting to heat up, humidity starting to gear up, we went to breakfast at Ann's, where we all started to discuss the agenda of the day—sightseeing, antiquing, and absorbing the town itself in a slightly different light than simply just a day at the races.

Strolling through the backstreets in town, checking out the local culture, we were surprised to come upon someone selling off some extraneous artifacts—commonly called garage sales today. We spent a few quid in picking up some little antiques and such. Going by the cemetery, we couldn't help but notice some of the dates on the tombstones from the late 1700s through the 1800s. As we strolled on the backstreets, we then decided to drive up to Union Avenue and do something we had never done before: check out the Racing Museum. We paid our admission and entered. I'm almost sure it was '72 because jockey Eric Guerin, and trainer Johnny Nerud of Tartan Stables, trainer of the fabulous and fast Dr. Fager, were to be inducted that year. Being that the first numbered oil painting I had ever done was of a chestnut mare with a white blaze and foal at her side, chowing down on the green grass, presumably of Bluegrass, Kentucky, I vividly remembered a great painting which is probably still in those archives. It was that of Sunny Jim Fitzsimmons, legendary trainer, under a broad elm sitting on a bench, speaking to a famous jockey, presumably Eddie Arcaro, with a Thoroughbred standing at an angle, discussing race strategy.

After gazing at all the memorabilia, we all stopped at the gift shop on our way out. Jimmy and I bought inexpensive money clips. The motif was that of a two-dollar American Totalisator machine–winning ticket ingrained in red. The ticket was a two-dollar win ticket on the no. 7 horse in the seventh race on July 7, 1977. If you're really sharp, you'll pick that up as six and not seven, realizing that Jimmy and I had made a pact to go to Belmont that day and bet seven dollars to win on the no. 7 horse, making it seven sevens ironically.

Years into the future, that day finally arrived, but we didn't go. Not because we didn't want to. It was because when we saw the overnight entries, we were unnerved by the fact that there were only six horses entered. Oh well, it was what it was. End of story.

3-6-9 Everything Is Mine

Once again, August arrived. Time for Saratoga and the four-week meet. We were going for the third time as married couples. Typically, we started out at the break of dawn, at 5:00 a.m. from Brooklyn/Long Island, quickly crossing the Throgs Neck and Tappan Zee bridges, hitting the thruway at Suffern, absolutely breaking the speed limit without much caution, and getting to our first coffee stop at the first Hot Shop as dawn was breaking with the sweet smell of late summer air. On our two-hundred-mile trek to the Thoroughbred Motel, we were, as usual, hoping to see Bill and his wife for our annual eight-dollars-per-day adjoining cabin rooms with an attached front porch. Usually arriving at 9:00 a.m., making necessary arrangements, keys in hand, Jimmy and I would park out front, bring the bags in, let the girls unpack and mosey over to the awninged picnic area to meet some of the old crowd should they be there, and have our usual coffee and jelly donuts graciously provided by Bill.

Year after year, usually it would be Angelo, the taxi driver from the Bronx and Jim, the writer for UPI not remembering names, occasionally a steeplechase jock, and one shifty-looking character coincidentally forgetting his name, but always having the Ragozin sheets in his hand, saying something as to the effect, "This is the best thing since sliced bread."

Within that first sixty to ninety minutes, as the girls were setting up the rooms, Jimmy and I, with *Tele*s in our hands and our preconceived notions about the daily doubles, began discussing the first two races with the guys. We typically went up at the beginning of the second week, and we all thought that someone was going to pull a fast one, and there was going to be a monster payoff the next day. Naturally, it had to be in a daily double. Back at that time, you only had daily doubles in the first two races; the third, fifth, and seventh were the only exotic bets taken. There were eight or ten of us in the group of punters, so we all decided that it had to be a monster daily double; four- or five-thousand-dollar payoff on a two-dollar daily double ducat. We all chipped in seventy or eighty dollars apiece to cover all combinations. That morning, not remembering which one of us went down early to place the bet, everything was covered long before noontime as the first race went off at one o'clock. We didn't win. The daily double paid some two to three hundred dollars, and we all lost forty to fifty dollars apiece. After the eighth race, the four of us decided we were going to go to the races at Green Mountain Racetrack. We wanted to get a head start on the crowd, because we heard if you get to Wally's in Rutland too late, they would be out of their fabulous prime rib. As we were traveling just outside of Saratoga going to Green Mountain, we heard the stretch call of the ninth race at Saratoga on the radio. What we didn't realize was that it happened to be the beginning of the trifecta initiation. We passed it up, not thinking of it; none of us ever gave it a thought. As it turned out that day in the last race, the ninth race, Squire Henry wins like a champ, paying some sixty odd dollars, followed up by a couple of other long shots, and the trifecta comes back and pays over sixty-four thousand dollars, the biggest payoff in such a bet ever at that time. We all looked at each other and said we knew there was going to be a big payoff—wrong race, wrong bet—but albeit we were right about one thing: it was the right day.

Every Dog Has His Day

Here it was again, the beginning of August 1974. The four of us—Jimmy and I and Marion and Lucy—would go up the first weekend of racing to Saratoga. That year, we decided to go up early Tuesday morning since there was no racing. On Monday evening, Jim called and asked if it was okay if his dad came with us. We were driving him up to the lake to see his friends and picking him up a couple of days later for the return to Long Island. Jim said, "Don't worry, he'll probably pick up breakfast, gas, and tolls." Jim, Lucy, and Jack rolled up at 5:00 a.m. outside our apartment in Rosedale. Throwing our luggage in the trunk, Jimmy asked, "Would you mind driving? I'm tired."

I said, "No problem. Give me the keys."

Jim sat shotgun and Jack sat in between the girls in the backseat with his racing form and his coffee mug. Jack looked a little flush as he always did, all six foot, two hundred and twenty-five pounds like a little Santa without the beard; although his cup, having a slight bit of condensation, said something like mimosa, not java. As we trekked north, I remembered dropping a quarter at the Throgs Neck bridge then once again at the Tappan Zee and pulling over at the first Hot Shop to pick up our coffee and donuts. Much to our surprise, Jack said, "You go ahead. I'm good."

We came back out, pulled up to the gas pumps, and filled the tank. And much to our surprise, Jack never reached in his pocket. A few hours later, getting up to Albany, once again Jack never reached in his pocket to pay the toll exiting the New York State Thruway. Now just thirty miles from Saratoga, we were going to get off at exit 13 to go to Ann's for breakfast. Jack noticed that we were getting off at the first exit and he said, "No, go past this exit and go up to the lake first, which is basically the next exit." And we did. Getting to Palmer's Maple Shade, we dropped Jack off at the cottage, went in for a few minutes, and Jack said, "So you'll call me when you're ready to go back?"

Jim said, "Yeah, no problem, Dad."

We backtracked to exit thirteen, went to the Thoroughbred Motel, checked in, and proceeded to Ann's for breakfast. I said to Jim, "What happened? No tolls, no gas, no coffee, no breakfast. Jack didn't pick up a thing."

Jim said, "Don't worry. He'll get it on the way back."

We stayed two nights and actually made a nice chunk of change at the races, had a few good meals, and a really good time. The second day, we called Jack and said we would be leaving after the day's races.

He said, "Fine, pick me up and talk to you tomorrow."

That Thursday after the races, we picked up Jack at the lake on Route 9 approaching the Northway. Jack said, "Go past the parkway. You can gas up and we'll get something to eat at Reds."

Jim said, "Reds? What's Reds?"

Jack said, "It's a little joint set off the road the other side of the parkway."

All five of us sat down and had a great dinner. When the bill came, the total was a whopping thirty dollars. I went to the men's room. Jim shortly followed, and when he caught me inside, he said, "Don't worry, my dad will pick up the bill while we're inside."

A couple of minutes later back at the table, there was the bill, the two girls, and Jack was at the bar talking to an old friend. Waiting about five minutes, Jack yelled across the bar to the table, "Aren't you knuckleheads ready yet? Let's go."

Jim and I split the bill. Jim said, "Don't worry, he'll get the gas."

Pulling up to the gas pump, Jack, reading the paper with his glasses down on his nose, didn't move a lick. Jimmy and I, outside the car, filled the tank. It wasn't a whole hell of a lot, only seven or eight dollars, gas being only about twenty-six, twenty-seven cents a gallon, but Jack never lifted a finger. Payback's a bitch. Jimmy and I had completely forgotten about the 1964 $213 daily double that Jack never collected because we forgot to put the bet in.

Caesar's Wish

Pennsylvanian Sally M. Gibson was waiting patiently for a yearling filly to be led to the sales ring at the Timonium Thoroughbred sales. Very happy to hear the gavel fall—going once, going twice, going three times, sold—the filly brought the sum of $12,000. With a smile on her face, she and her husband, John, approached her new trainer and confidant, Richard Small. After all, it was not only he but also his mother, Jane, sister of Hall of Fame trainer Sid Watters, who identified this late May 30 foal with correct confirmation and looked at her as a prospective good one. You see, the $12,000 price tag was probably based upon her being such a late foal. Looking at her breeding, her lightly raced sire, Proudest Roman—four wins in five starts, with earnings over $130,000—and being a granddaughter of the great miler Never Bend, owned by Cain Hoy Stables and an undefeated entry in the 1963 Kentucky Derby, now made her look like a steal.

This story takes precedence in this book. She developed into quite the amazing filly, as a matter of fact. As the story goes on, you will see why. It was 1978. I was at Belmont Park, New York, reading the racing form. I wanted to take a look at a filly from Maryland named Caesar's Wish. As I was handicapping the race, a number of things didn't seem to fit. At that time, I was somewhat unfamiliar with Richard Small and his rider, Danny Wright. I never heard of them before but was always looking to explore further. I noticed the filly had been well traveled from Maryland, New York, Kentucky, and back again now to New York and being shipped in from Maryland—this had to make a good handicapper take a deeper look. I thought she must have quality since she had been entered in the feature, the Mother Goose for three-year-old fillies. Back in those days, unlike today, there weren't as many horses shipped in to race against top-quality New York horses. Quite the opposite, they sort of take the high road and ship elsewhere against weaker competition in an effort to make easy money.

Since I usually got to the races early, I had enough time to examine all and even be in the paddock area to get a visual. As the betting opened, she seemed to be one of the outsiders on the tote board at 11-1. It caught my attention. Notoriously, most good handicappers have the knowledge that early money coming in on a horse early and late money coming in late on a horse were both notable. I took a second look both at the tote board and the racing form and really couldn't believe this filly was about to go off at an overlay beyond belief. I decided to take a closer look, not knowing what I would see in the paddock area—the odds went down to 10-1 and then back up to 11, again to 10, back and forth. While in the saddling area, the filly looked fine. I couldn't understand it since she had won most of her races. And from what I could see, she was either odds-on favorite, 9-5, 2-1, 5-2 almost every trip.

As the horses were led out of the paddock area into the tunnel, through the tunnel, and led out to the post parade, the filly still looked absolutely solid. Since I've been known to wager a few quid in my day, and being satisfied that she looked great, I went to the windows; and to be honest, I can't recall if I dropped ten or twenty on her nose. I looked up at the tote board with only four or five minutes to post, and her odds started to dramatically tumble—a good sign. The crowd seemed to agree this horse was a winner. A few minutes later, as the gate opened, she was running easily, the fractions were fast, and her rider didn't even seem to have her on the bit. A thought went through my head for an instant back in the day, when we didn't know if a rider was any good or was a bug boy. We used to say that the trainer would put him in the saddle and strap him on.

As I watched the race unfold, I couldn't believe my eyes. Danny who? She was opening the lead, running a hole in the wind, and came home under a hand ride the easy winner. Caesar's Wish and Danny Wright, easiest of winners and a story to remember, breaking the great Ruffian's stakes record of 1:47.60.

If that's not a story worth mentioning, you have to hear this. I can't remember the date exactly, but it couldn't have been more than a day or two, and certainly within that week, I noticed a small byline dealing with this shipper that came in from Maryland and ran off with the Mother Goose. Being thirty-seven years later and trying to recall the story about this captioned article attesting to Caesar's Wish and an eventful trip to Belmont Park, the byline appearing in the racing form on one of the inside pages was a story about Caesar's Wish. It caught my eye since I made money on the race and the winner, and always curious about the reasons behind why a horse such as Caesar's Wish and running a quality record-shattering race, I had to read on. Truth or fiction, I know not, but certainly worthy of mention. The article goes on to tell of Caesar's Wish being vanned from Baltimore to Belmont Park. Along the way and for whatever reason, I do not know the truck with the horse trailer with Caesar's Wish inside, pulled to the side or off the Jersey Turnpike, and the horse was backed out of the trailer naturally on a short shank, either to relax or feed the horse possibly halfway through the trip. In a flash, the horse bolted for a nearby meadow and ran off, and fifteen or twenty minutes later, the handlers gathered her back up and calmed her down to reload her. Obviously, they decided to move forward and continue on their trip to Belmont Park that morning, and the rest was history.

Albeit the article was written and published in the *Daily Racing Form* (I know, I read it), factual or not, I had to tell this story. I've done everything humanly possible to corroborate, as many of you now know, so I've decided to go on and tell the story, and I will make this simple statement. Should it turn out to be true, I believe I have just seen the likes of Pegasus reincarnated, and those in the know, such as Danny Wright, her rider, I'm sure would agree.

DANNY WRIGHT
Journeyman

Danny in his Riding days

Mike Sassin, chart caller for Equibase on left
Danny Wright, chief steward at Charlestown race track WVa 2016

Wun Little Wabbit

1979

It was a cloudy, dreary, rainy day, late morning at Aqueduct Racetrack. Marshall Cassidy, race caller for the track, was going over his program and racing form. His main objective was to deal with certain idiosyncrasies that would allow him to easily recognize every particular horse in the field. By making an association with the animals, he could quickly and correctly identify each horse at any stage of the race. This afforded him the ability to translate his thoughts into the words necessary to flawlessly enunciate and allow the fans to understand the development of the race at all times. He would take a number of facets into consideration, starting with the horse's name; his post position number; the owner's colors; the color, size, and any particular mannerisms of the horse itself; the jockey and his riding style; and any other physical characteristics that might separate one jock from another. He would then go to his racing form and handicap the race itself, trying to understand how the race would develop. As he handicapped the race, he would try to establish the front running speed in the race, anticipating which horses would control the race on the front end and if there would be a speed duel and how fast the fractions for the first quarter and a half would go. He then would see whom he believed the trackers were in the race, how many if any, and approximately where they would be in the early stages of the race. These trackers would be the horses that broke well, but not fast enough to be caught up on the front in the early stages of the race. He would then anticipate which of the horses (again, if any) would be the laggards in the early stages and, hopefully, would make a late come-from-behind type of move that could eventually bring them to the winner's circle. Knowing this in advance of the race gave Marshall a decided edge in what to anticipate, and if he were correct, he could then make an astute race call, should racing luck be on his side. Racing luck—meaning a clean break out of the gate, not a heck of a lot of bumping, crowding, or any misfortune that commonly occurred in many races. With his guns loaded, he was preparing himself in a very short time frame to envision the outcome of the race, make the call, and go on for eight other races on the agenda.

Marshall was extremely adept at calling a race, which was quite a task in all the confusion as ten or twelve Thoroughbreds would break from the gate, and in a minute and twelve seconds of jostling and bumping and struggling for position as they thundered for the finish line. He had a certain stoic professionalism common in his job. He seemed to be able to do this in such a confident manner that it was hard to believe that it wasn't a rerun of the race itself.

A quintessential race caller of his day, rather than the auctioneer's famed style of jargon, *his* account seemed to follow a Shakespearian flow. He was brash and confident at the same time, very similar to a champion Thoroughbred that would be on edge with some nervous energy. But as soon as the gates opened, it would settle into a beautifully extended, long, ground-gobbling stride.

Marshall, his own humor more wry than mirthful, had been waiting for a few months for a perfect opportunity to expose this particular wit to the public and his peers. In anticipation of the right timing, he believed he could pull off a race call involving a certain Thoroughbred with an awful lot of fun, in a race call à la Elmer Fudd that could go down in the annals of racing and be remembered by many—certainly this guy.

There was a sort of nondescript Thoroughbred named *What a Rabbit*, a horse that rarely won or even ran consistently well. He was a three- or four-year-old that had lost nine or ten consecutive races but is, in fact, the key element in this humorous story. Fitting in with his plan, Marshall made a study of this horse and his running style for a number of months. He took a great interest and probably put in more handicapping than he normally would for any given horse. He noticed that this horse basically had no speed at all, and that he would occasionally put in a less than effective closing punch at certain times.

As Marshall handicapped the races that *What a Rabbit* had run in, it seemed that in shorter sprint races, he would occasionally run well at the end of the race. As he continued further, he found that the horse was totally ineffective in route races, and his breeding indicated that was not his forte. As Marshall's study went further, he did notice that when *What a Rabbit* went into a positive cycle, he would put together two or three better-than-average races, showing his late closing kick. In the back of Marshall's mind, he would wait for the opportune time to make his stand. In the past months, through the previous races by *What a Rabbit*, Marshall was correct, and *What a Rabbit* had not run the race of his life. But on this day, as Marshall handicapped *What a Rabbit's* previous two races, in which he turned in two fairly consistent late running moves, it seemed to set him up for his third race of a good cycle, and the timing now seemed ideal to let loose with his humor.

Now Marshall would have to wait a couple of hours to see if everything looked to be right in the post parade for the sixth race and if the horse's demeanor and physical condition looked to be a positive. To pull off this race call, he had but one shot and one shot only. If everything went right, he would start his anticipated call moments after the break of the race, continue on, and be judged brilliant by all; if not, everything would collapse and fall like the Roman empire, and he would end up with egg on his face. Not only did the horse have to run well, but continue on and win in an absolutely convincing manner—a tall order of the day and saving the possibility of total embarrassment. Everything seemed to be going right, and for some reason, it seemed like a premonition, almost as if he had a crystal ball. Marshall had an air of confidence as he said to himself, sooner or later, the time would come; and hopefully, today was the day.

Approximately nine or ten minutes previously, he was correct and didn't utter a word, but the odds were growing short, and as in any theory, it had to happen like flipping a coin. What were the odds that tails would come up another time? He sat back and pondered the forthcoming event. He knew he had to make an astute observation and react quickly (almost instantly and subconsciously) if, in fact, today was the day. So he sat back, sipped a cup of coffee, put the thoughts in the back of his head, and turned his racing form to another page, another race, and went on with other matters of the day.

Hours before the race, little did Marshall know it would all come together on this day. With a few races in the day, this race with What a Rabbit was gradually coming closer. Thirty minutes prior to race time, Marshall went off to see What a Rabbit settle in and be saddled for his race, watching with an astute eye, registering little things such as the condition of his coat; movement of the horse; ear movement picking up sounds from the crowd, indicating its alertness; and the general demeanor of the horse itself. After studying this horse today and a number of times in the past, Marshall had the feeling that considering how he ran the last two times in his current cycle, this could be the day he could pull off the upset win. The two most recent races indicated his style of running from far off the pace and finishing strongly both times but falling short by a number of lengths, finishing fifth and sixth respectively with a big middle move and hanging in the late stages of each race. The fact was What a Rabbit—entered in this race today, a slightly cheaper claiming race—would have a great chance of winning against lesser-quality horses.

As the horses were led onto the track ten minutes prior to the race, in the post parade and subsequent warm-up, Marshall began to study, further noticing What a Rabbit's ears were pricking, head bowed, kind of full of himself, nuzzling the lead pony. What a Rabbit appeared noticeably different than in his prior races and had a self-assured confidence about himself. Now after the post parade, the horses were turned around back up the stretch, around the turn, and down the backstretch in the normal clockwise direction opposite that of the direction the race would be run in, leading all the horses to the starting gate being prepared for the start of the race. Marshall, with binoculars in hand, made his way toward the microphones and his vantage point to make the call of the race. He knew if this was the day, he'd have to make an instantaneous decision to make his long-anticipated call of this race.

With one minute to post time, Marshall went over this quickly in his mind. He had to recognize that since What a Rabbit was a dead closer that it would only work provided he broke poorly near the back of the pack. Seeing that the horse looked confident and prepared to run the race of his life in the prior post parade, Marshall could begin his call. Trying to anticipate the development of the race and for it to come up flawlessly, Marshall saw the race in his mind's eye and began. What a Rabbit broke poorly, sat ninth and last, and ran down the backstretch.

He started to gather steam, passed two horses, and angled toward the rail. He got through running on the rail, passing another two. Now raging full of run, he went wide and won the race by two!

Approaching the gate, the handlers started moving the horses into the gate one by one. Everything seemed to be calm; none of the horses acted up. They loaded the last few and approached post time. The starter kept a watchful eye. He watched for any would-be problems, any horses that might act up, since his job was to assure a fair and equitable start to the race; after that, anything goes. He lifted his starter's gun—which, in this day and age, was no longer a gun. In fact, it was an electronic starting device, a button that simultaneously allowed the bell to ring and the gates to burst open for a perfect start. Seeing everything was perfect for the start, the starter raised his arm, pushed the button, and the gates opened. The bell rang, and the race was on.

In a flash, a mili-moment, Marshall recognized that that this was it. Everything in the universe came together. He knew he was right and began his call. It flowed like the famous scene from *Gone with the Wind* when Rhett Butler stood on the steps of Tara, looked down on Scarlett O'Hara, and said "Frankly, my dear, I don't give a damn" and walked off. In an Oscar-winning performance, Marshall's lips opened, his voice rose, and the words began to flow: "What a Wabbit is wunning last, winding his way like a fweight twain, angling toward the wail, picking up horses one by one, swings wide past the grandstand, winning the wace by one."

Phewwww! He did it, he did it. Everything came together like a premonition. I think Marshall was in more of a lather than the horse after the race. An ordinary day just seemed to become extraordinary. I salute Marshall Cassidy, the quintessential race caller, unequaled bar none (or, possibly, one Freddy "Cappy" Capossela), clapping vigorously from atop the grandstand. Well done, well done.

Funny Now

Early in my life, I was drawn to the Thoroughbred. It was visually magnificent, like poetry in motion, long striding on the track. I immediately knew I had no chance of escaping. Keeping my family in the dark, though not intentionally, my friend Jimmy and I went to the races every Saturday. Long after everyone knew I was going to the races, I decided to take my parents for a day at Belmont. It was a summer day in the late seventies, sunny and warm, not a cloud in the sky—a perfect racing day. We arrived after the second race, midafternoon. My parents were awed by the majesty of it all. When the horses came out for the third race post parade, we were sitting in the clubhouse. Eight entered; my mother, surveying the field, said, "What do I do?"

I said, "Look at them all. See which one you like, and then I'll walk you up to the windows to make your bet."

With about ten minutes to post as the horses walked past the grandstand, my mother said, "I see the one I want to bet. I love the black one."

I began looking through the field of eight. I saw two or three chestnuts, one gray, and the other four or five were all bays—nothing dark at all. I didn't see a black. Basically, blacks were uncommon. I said to my mother, "I don't see one."

She said, "Right there, right there. Don't you see?"

I said, "No." I reiterated three or four times. No.

She then said, "The one with the red on all the hooves."

I looked and I said, "Ma, the ones with the numbers on their backs." The red on all their hooves were the red socks on the outrider's pony, a smallish black with red socks that I didn't even realize was out there.

After all, I was looking at the racehorses. By the time we got to bet the race, my mother had picked her numbers, but we were shut out. And, naturally, her horse won.

Now a couple of years earlier, it was Christmas Eve. Everything opened late, except the banks. I got a call from my brother, somewhat of a rare call. And as far as I knew, he rarely played the horses. He said to me, "I want to get a bet in. Can you get a bet in for me?"

I said, "I'll see what I can do."

"I just got a tip from a friend of mine who knows the jockey. I want to bet a one-hundred-dollar daily double."

I said, "Whoa! Are you sure?"

He said, "Yeah. I want to wheel the no. 1 horse with everything in the second race."

Thinking it was for the next day—Christmas—I said, "I don't think there's racing tomorrow."

He said, "No, it's the double at Roosevelt."

I don't remember if it was Roosevelt or Yonkers, but I did say, "There's eight horses in those, and that's $800. And it's the trotters, not the flats." I concluded, "The only thing I can do is put it in through OTB."

He said, "I don't care. Can you do it?"

I said, "It's Christmas Eve. I don't have eight hundred in cash, and the banks are closed."

There were no ATMs in those days. I emphatically said, "No. Anybody that gets a tip from a friend of a jockey who is riding a trotter doesn't know what they're talking about." If he had told me the driver of the trotter, I might have thought differently; but since he hadn't, I flatly refused, telling him, "You're saving money, not expanding on the reasoning." I had Christmas shopping to do.

Next day, I find the first race. The 1 wins, pays eight in change; and as luck had it, the no. 8 horse got up at the wire, beat the no. 2 horse, the odds-on favorite at 37-1, for a daily-double payoff at slightly over $800. A hundred-dollar double pays slightly over forty *g*'s; a mere bag of shells. Needless to say, my brother didn't speak to me for a long time.

The next and last time I took my mother to the races was in Hauppauge, New York, at the off-track racing facility. Maybe you thought I had learned my lesson, bringing family to the races. Nooooo, I forgot which race it was, but it was a two-year-old race in 1988. Eight going in a maiden special weight sprint, only the no. 4 horse had one try on the track. The no. 2 was fluctuating between 2-5 and 3-5; the no. 4 horse, if I'm correct, was 2 or 3–1; and the rest were pretty much double digits. I explained to my mother that I did not think the no. 2 horse could lose, and I said, "I don't think the no. 4 horse can run anything but second." I was salivating. I was looking at a one-way exacta 2/4, maybe a little back up 4/2—maybe $40/10 just in case. My mother said, "What should I bet?"

I said, "Bet twenty dollars to win on the 2," thinking she would turn twenty dollars into thirty dollars. Mistake number 1 was telling her. Mistake number 2 was letting her go on her own to place the bet. I got my bet in; she came back, and we sat down to watch the race. The connections on the two were impeccable. As the race unfolded, the no. 2 horse, fairly quickly, got the lead; and down the stretch, the no. 4 horse made a futile attempt to run at the winner, clearly second best. The rest of the field spread out in the stretch. My mother jumped up, declaring, "I won! I won! I won!"

I felt good that I gave her a winner. The exacta came back just about five dollars. I turned forty dollars into about one hundred dollars, and I was happy. I looked at my mother and said, "You won! How much did you put on it?"

She said, "I did what you told me to do. I put twenty dollars to win on him."

If memory serves me right, that day, the Ogden Phipps–owned, Shug McGaughey–trained *Easy Goer*, ridden by Pat Day, won off by four in hand first time out. I brought my mother to the window to collect on our bets. She pulled out a handful of tickets, and I said, "You didn't have to put in a bunch of two-dollar tickets."

She said, "I didn't. I told him twenty dollars to win."

And I said, "Give me the tickets. Let me see what you did."

Absolutely thrilled that she won, she handed them over to me, and I saw she put twenty dollars to win on every horse in the race—a $160 bet—and she was giddy as she cashed in approximately thirty dollars. I rolled my eyes and let her enjoy the moment, never again to be revisited.

Reminiscing, I thought I might tell you a cute little story about my friend, Jim, and his father, Jack. And I might as well throw in his brother Robert. When you speak to him, he speaks somewhat proudly of his little Carvel escapade. For those who do not know the name Carvel, this is a soft-serve ice cream with a walk-up window, basically a

Northeast company and, might I say, pretty good ice cream. When we were younger, we had one in our town. Best I can remember, Jimmy and his younger brother, Robert, were about eight and six years old at the time. Jimmy loved Carvel. Not having any money, he went to his father's dresser drawer, and lo and behold, he opened a cigar box and pulled out a couple of pennies. He walked down to Carvel, proceeded to the window, and put up his two pennies. He said to the young guy at the window, "Can I get a Carvel for this?" The server looked down and hesitated for ten or fifteen seconds and finally said to him, "I guess I can give you a small one."

Jimmy walked away happy as a pig. Two days later, he went back to the box, pulled out four pennies, grabbed his brother, and said, "Come with me. We're going to get Carvel." He was hoping the guy would give him two Carvels—one for him and one for his brother. Robert, being only six, questioned his brother. "Can we really get two ice creams?"

Jim said, "I hope so." They got to Carvel, and he asked the guy again as he placed four cents on the counter. The guy looked at him and said, "Yeah, sure, kids, but they will be two small ones." He handed them two big ones, and the kids were in their glory. And he said, "Go ahead and enjoy."

Every day or so, when Jimmy came home and his father never said anything, this just emboldened him. Jimmy didn't give it a thought. It was only a couple of pennies, and with his father being a pretty good guy, it wouldn't really matter. This went on almost the entire summer.

Jimmy had brought his brother Robert with him virtually every other day. About a week before school opened, Jimmy's mother and father were about to take them for school clothes, and he looked in the drawer. Casually putting some cash in his pocket, he opened the cigar box and almost had a massive coronary! His face totally flushed. He came out and shouted, "Who's been in my drawer?"

Nobody said a word. His father demanded to know who had been in the cigar box. And he added, "If I don't get an answer right now, none of you are eating. And you're not doing anything but going to school, and that's that."

King James finally fessed up, and his father said, "What in the hell were you thinking?"

Half smart-ass and crying at the same time, Jimmy explained, "It was just a few pennies, Dad."

His father shook his head, took a few minutes to gather himself up, thought about it, and said, "Those were two-and-a-half-dollar gold pieces."

In 1951, that was virtually a king's ransom. Jimmy accidentally plundered about 150 of those gold pieces, leaving at least forty or fifty, thinking his father wouldn't miss them. After all, they were only pennies, and he really wouldn't get that crazy.

So the Carvel summer was over. Since I'm good and I can run the numbers, that was approximately 150 two-and-a-half-dollar gold pieces, or an approximate face value of $375. To put it in 2010 terms—gold being near the top of the market at $1,900 an ounce—those gold pieces would convert to slightly over $14,000. Jimmy's father must have rolled over. To this day, we both laugh about it. Now remembering this, connecting the dots, now I know why Jimmy's father absconded with that two-dollar winning ticket on *Daring Heart* paying $214.

Fasig-Tipton Saratoga Yearling Sales

It was the summer of '81, the first year of Reagan's presidency. Interest rates were through the roof, the dollar was decimated, and foreign currencies were rocketing. Europeans and other foreigners came to Saratoga to plunder the Fasig-Tipton Thoroughbred yearling sales in early August. They would ship their bounty of extraordinarily well bred fillies and colts back to Europe and other venues and develop and improve the quality of bloodstock in their homelands. This took place before the catchphrase Reaganomics existed.

Early August 1981 at dusk, in the cool of the evening, this spectacular event was about to commence after the last races of the afternoon. As the crowd flowed from the clubhouse and grandstand areas and the track emptied after the day of racing, race fans would gather at their local haunts, taverns, and restaurants. A smaller and elite group of fans would contemplate attending the Fasig-Tipton sales. With an air of anticipation, automobiles started to arrive in the grassy parking lots off Union Avenue, adjacent to the barn areas. The rotunda of deep, rich mahogany and glass, visible to all, was where the sale of the Thoroughbreds would take place in due time. As the cars filled the parking areas, later arrivals would then have to park on the streets, as far as the eye could see. Individuals and groups leaving their autos, joined by people leaving restaurants and taverns, all targeted and focused on entering the sales area, some stopping at the office to pick up catalogues and bidding passes for the evening's event. As the chatter heightened with horse lingo, many of those people would begin to take in the sights. As they approached a grassy area, you could not help but notice an easel with an oil painting, depicting a race with a background of the grandstand at Saratoga, by Jennes Cortez. This framed piece of art was presented aesthetically and also had a $2,500 price tag attached.

Looking farther, it was impossible not to notice a number of yellow-and-white tents large enough to accommodate from one to two hundred people. Lines formed in front of temporary bars, serviced by waiters in tuxedos, taking orders for exotic cocktails. All were rubbing elbows, and the banter went on as owners, trainers, bloodstock agents, aristocrats, dignitaries, and everyday folk gathered for one sole purpose—the Thoroughbred racehorse, his breeding and conformation—looking to catch lightning in a bottle. Some hoped to come away with a bargain price of $20,000 or $30,000, and to more fortunate others, a regally bred animal who could go for numbers rising in the millions. All were seeking fame and fortune, with thoughts of the Kentucky Derby and the other Triple Crown events. As the evening continued and the auction bidding began and the gavel came down time and again, ladies in broad-brimmed straw hats and flowery frilly cotton-print dresses were sipping cocktails and speaking with one another while the men strolled off concerned with the evening's business, planning their strategies, holding their catalogues, discussing the breeding of certain hip numbers, and anticipating where a winning bid would make them the proud owner of a world-beater.

In the early eighties, winning bids for the regally bred individuals were rising to the point of getting out of hand. Bids that commonly, in prior years, would rise to the hundreds of thousands of dollars were escalating into the millions. That evening, the sales toppers had gone to between three and four million. This occurred because of the devaluation in the dollar and the strengthening of foreign currencies. The British pound, French franc, German mark, and the Arab oil money allowed the Europeans and Arabs to cherry-pick the cream of the crop of the Thoroughbred-breeding industry, ship back to their homelands, improve the caliber of their breeding industry, and at the same time, decimating the American breeding industry all in one fell swoop.

Only a rare, well-heeled group of individuals could afford to play this game. Well into the evening, they all began to notice that their purchasing agents were making winning bids on a large number of handsome and well-bred equines. These individuals, who sipped cocktails and allowed their agents to carry on the bidding process, began to think twice; they conferred and developed a solution to these astronomical bidding practices. They decided that since they were outbidding almost the entire crowd, there had to be a way to establish a saner and less costly way of accomplishing an equal end result. In my opinion, they must have created a solution to banging heads and somehow refrain from bidding against one another and needlessly driving up the prices. This individual can make a broad assumption, since I was not there at these cocktail-sipping meetings, that they handled this matter very astutely. Robert Sangster of the British soccer pools; Peter Brandt, American entrepreneur; Sheikh Mohammed bin Rashid Al Maktoum, businessman and dignitary; and Eugene Klein, NFL franchise owner, all shook hands and said adieu, thus changing forever American and international Thoroughbred racing.

There was Wayne Lukas, trainer of some of the best Thoroughbreds, in his broad-brimmed ten-gallon white cowboy hat, speaking with some individuals. And across the way, there was Jack Van Berg, trainer of the famous Alysheba, speaking with other people and eating a frankfurter, walking quickly to check out the conformation of another hip number about to enter the sales ring. As the gavel came down time and again throughout the evening, horses were led off by winning bidders to enter life in a different barn with different owners and trainers. The business of auctioning these horses came to a close, waiting for another day tomorrow and the day after. So the day's business was done, and the Fasig-Tipton yearling sales came to a close that evening, about midnight, at Saratoga. Life would be incomplete without this experience and the pageantry and the charm of Saratoga in August.

THE
SARATOGA
SALE

SONGBIRD ECLIPSE AWARD STELLAR WIND

TEPIN AMERICAN PHAROAH

SELECTED YEARLINGS

AUGUST 8-9, 6:30PM

 FasigTipton

Saratoga Faisig-Tipton Yearling Sales August 2016

Above in walking ring, two year old Roan Colt by
2007 Kentucky Derby Winner Street Sense

Below, Hip #4 in auction ring, being sold

Consigned by Bluewater Sales LLC, Agent XXI

Barn 4

Gray or Roan Colt

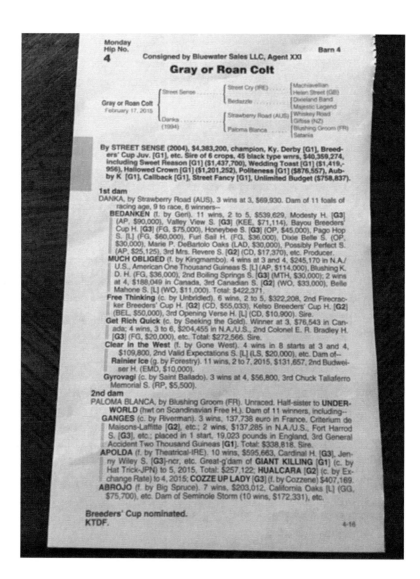

		Street Cry (IRE)	Machiavellian
Street Sense			Helen Street (GB)
	Bedazzle		Ocean Crest Band
			Majestic Legend
Danka		Strawberry Road (AUS)	Whiskey Road
(1994)			Giftisa (NZ)
	Paloma Blanca		Blushing Groom (FR)
			Sataria

Gray or Roan Colt
February 17, 2015

By STREET SENSE (2004), $4,383,200, champion, Ky. Derby [G1], Breed-
ers' Cup Juv. [G1], etc. Sire of 6 crops, 45 black type wnrs, $40,359,274,
including Sweet Reason [G1] ($1,437,700), Wedding Toast [G1] ($1,419,-
956), Hallowed Crown [G1] ($1,201,252), Politeness [G1] ($876,557), Aub-
by K [G1], Callback [G1], Street Fancy [G1], Unlimited Budget ($758,837).

1st dam
DANKA, by Strawberry Road (AUS). 3 wins at 3, $69,930. Dam of 11 foals of
racing age, 9 to race, 6 winners—
BEDANKEN (f. by Geri). 11 wins, 2 to 5, $539,629, Modesty H. [G3]
(AP, $90,000), Valley View S. [G3] (KEE, $71,114), Bayou Breeders'
Cup H. [G3] (FG, $75,000), Honeybee S. [G3] (OP, $45,000), Pago Hop
S. [L] (FG, $60,000), Furl Sail H. (FG, $36,000), Dixie Belle S. (OP,
$30,000), Marie P. DeBartolo Oaks (LAD, $30,000), Possibly Perfect S.
(AP, $25,125), 3rd Mrs. Revere S. [G2] (CD, $17,370), etc. Producer.
MUCH OBLIGED (f. by Kingmambo). 4 wins at 3 and 4, $245,170 in N.A./
U.S., American One Thousand Guineas S. [L] (AP, $114,000), Blushing K.
D. H. (FG, $36,000), 2nd Boiling Springs S. [G3] (MTH, $30,000); 2 wins
at 4, $188,049 in Canada, 3rd Canadian S. [G2] (WO, $33,000), Belle
Mahone S. [L] (WO, $11,000). Total: $422,371.
Free Thinking (c. by Unbridled). 6 wins, 2 to 5, $322,208, 2nd Firecrac-
ker Breeders' Cup H. [G2] (CD, $55,033), Kelso Breeders' Cup H. [G2]
(BEL, $50,000), 3rd Opening Verse H. [L] (CD, $10,900). Sire.
Get Rich Quick (c. by Seeking the Gold). Winner at 3, $76,543 in Can-
ada; 4 wins, 3 to 6, $204,455 in N.A./U.S., 2nd Colonel E. R. Bradley H.
[G3] (FG, $20,000), etc. Total: $272,566. Sire.
Clear in the West (f. by Gone West). 4 wins in 8 starts at 3 and 4,
$109,800, 2nd Valid Expectations S. [L] (LS, $20,000), etc. Dam of—
Rainier Ice (g. by Forestry). 11 wins, 2 to 7, 2015, $131,657, 2nd Budwei-
ser H. (EMD, $10,000).
Gyrovagi (c. by Saint Ballado). 3 wins at 4, $56,800, 3rd Chuck Taliaferro
Memorial S. (RP, $5,500).

2nd dam
PALOMA BLANCA, by Blushing Groom (FR). Unraced. Half-sister to UNDER-
WORLD (hwt on Scandinavian Free H.). Dam of 11 winners, including—
GANGES (c. by Riverman). 3 wins, 137,738 euro in France, Criterium de
Maisons-Laffitte [G2], etc.; 2 wins, $137,285 in N.A./U.S., Fort Harrod
S. [G3], etc.; placed in 1 start, 19,023 pounds in England, 3rd General
Accident Two Thousand Guineas [G1]. Total: $338,818. Sire.
APOLDA (f. by Theatrical-IRE). 10 wins, $595,663, Cardinal H. [G3], Jen-
ny Wiley S. [G3]-ncr, etc. Great-g'dam of GIANT KILLING [G1] (c. by
Hat Trick-JPN) to 5, 2015. Total: $257,122. HUALCARA [G2] (c. by Ex-
change Rate) to 4, 2015; COZZE UP LADY [G3] (f. by Cozzene) $407,169.
ABROJO (f. by Big Spruce). 7 wins, $203,012, California Oaks [L] (GG,
$75,700), etc. Dam of Seminole Storm (10 wins, $172,331), etc.

Breeders' Cup nominated.
KTDF.

4-16

The Vision

In Thoroughbred racing, there are many adages, but one comes to mind as one of the most prominent. I don't recall who first said it, but it goes, "When breeding Thoroughbreds, you breed the best to the best and hope for the best." With that cliché in mind, in the early eighties, John Gaines—remembered as the owner of Gainesway Farm located in the Bluegrass region of Kentucky, often considered the birthplace of Thoroughbred racing—had the vision to gather in one venue over a weekend in the mid fall the best Thoroughbreds to sort out the champion of each division to determine the Eclipse Award winners of the year. In 1984, the vision came to fruition. "They" called it the Breeders' Cup. This event not only attracted American horses but also international horses, and it became a global event.

Many people thought this Breeders' Cup would eventually surpass the Triple Crown races of the spring as the premiere racing event of the year. Now some thirty years later, that has not necessarily been the case, at least in my opinion. I still see the Triple Crown races as the premiere events of the year. Some can argue otherwise, but let me explain. At first glance, sure, the Breeders' Cup events end the year, late October to early November, pulling together all the year's major races, winners, exciting racing throughout the year, creating a mosaic and establishing all the Eclipse Award winners for each division and establishing Horse of the Year honors.

Now let's just remember, every spring, all horses have turned a year older as they all have the same birthday, and that is January 1 for all intents and purposes. Obviously, all two-year-olds, even the two-year-old juvenile champion of the previous year has turned three. These three-year-olds will be this year's crop eligible to run in the Triple Crown events. And the general rule of thumb is the Eclipse Award–winning two-year-old is pretty much defined as either the favorite or one of the favorites for the Kentucky Derby, the first event in the Triple Crown. So in effect, on the contrary, I say you have to make a decision—what comes first, the chicken or the egg? In the previous year, the Breeders' Cup, the egg has hatched, the chicken was developing, and the Triple Crown races still trumped the Breeders' Cup. I don't really know how long this will be, for in the future there may be a change in the leadership category. But at this point, I don't see it that way.

In the beginning of the calendar year, I viewed it as a new start. Let's say a rebirth every year for what will unfold, what dramas will evolve going into the spring, and anticipation for what I considered the race of races—"The Run for the Roses"—on the first Saturday in May. On that Saturday in Kentucky late afternoon, when the bugler calls and you hear the announcement of "Riders up," and the horses parade in front of the grandstand to "My Old Kentucky Home," it will be just a matter of minutes until the bell rings, and simultaneously, the gates open and the race caller will say, "We're off for the 141st running of the Kentucky Derby." I will add to that, obviously it's off to this year's Triple Crown. The Run for the Roses—the Kentucky Derby—still generates to the top of the list when speaking of the epitome of Thoroughbred racing. For all intents and purposes, you can reiterate all the clichés that ever have surfaced speaking of this very race, and they all pale when you step back a moment and realize it is the greatest two minutes in sports. I have learned in my many years that you can speak with anyone, sports-minded or not on that first Saturday in May, late afternoon, early evening, and you'd be astounded. Anyone you speak with—from any walk of life, male, female, young, or old—will be speaking about some aspect of the Kentucky Derby. It will be one of the most frequent questions you will hear; and of course, you will be asked your opinion on whether or not we have a Triple Crown winner coming.

California Dreamin'

In the mid-'80s, after vacationing in the hot and humid Florida weather five to ten years prior, we had decided that warm, dry desert weather was our cup of tea. Not only that, but the allure of Thoroughbred racing, training, owning, and breeding, and the knowledge of the race game was something we were yearning to attempt. Seeking housing and real estate and accommodating Thoroughbreds was our goal in the mid-'80s. We ventured a trip into the Rancho California, Temecula area in Southern California, looking for an ideal location. Marion and I, and our sons, James and Brian, vacationed that year, checking the area out. We accidentally stumbled upon a new area that was being built up in the aforementioned area. While riding down De Portola Road, which ran throughout the Temecula area, we accidentally ran across Jack Klugman's ranch, made famous by his horse Jacklin Klugman, running third in the 1980 Kentucky Derby and just down the road from Raintree Ranch, owned in a partnership by actor Dennis Weaver of *Gunsmoke* fame.

While we were there, we noticed a For Sale sign on a beautiful hacienda on a hilltop on five acres with some horses on the grounds. We all approached, rang the doorbell, and we were greeted by a gentleman and we struck up a conversation. He asked if we wanted to see the grounds and his breeding facility and the horses in the corrals. Before I get to that, let me paint you a picture of this beautiful abode. We entered into a very large, open floor with a pool table in the middle of the room, with furniture beautifully decorated around the large venue, with three bedrooms, a butler's pantry, a large eat-in kitchen, breakfast room, and dining room. The walls were lined with Fred Stone paintings and collector's plates and art work. It was simply astonishing. Across from the entranceway on the far area where the dining room lied was an entire wall of glass with sliding doors, entering a beautiful railed terrace, overlooking an exquisite in-ground pool and cabanas. After asking us if we'd like a cool drink, he said, "Now let me show you around the grounds."

Somewhat attached to one end of the sprawling ranch was an immaculate brand-new, six-stall breeding barn. We walked past the pool behind the breeding barn and came to a large eight-car garage. We entered and he showed us four or five beautiful vintage autos—his real affinity. I said, "So why are you dealing with Thoroughbreds?"

He simply said, "Have to pay the bills."

We went on and he showed us two, two-and-a-half acre pens in the rear and another one to the side, the same size. All these pens accommodated approximately eighteen mares. Alongside one area, he had a couple of stallions. All these mares were either in foal or about to be bred. All this and the home sat on ten acres, asking price of half a million. Alongside was a vacant five-acre parcel, which would accommodate twice as many horses. The absentee owner was asking fifty thousand. Before we left, he led me to believe that his price was negotiable and that his neighbor's price was also negotiable. I felt very assured. If I offered $450,000 for both, I probably would have come up with the deal. We were all blown away by the majesty of the property in this beautiful area of Southern California. We went on to buy something else, but that property today stands at ten to fifteen million without the extra acreage.

Luck of the Irish

Sometime in late 1986, a fall day, I was sitting at my desk at 214 Madison Avenue, one of Ferdinand Marcos's holdings. Midday rolled around, and in walked a young-looking slender dark-haired lady about noontime, asking if I'd allow her to look around the store. I said "surely." Fifteen minutes rolled on, and she approached my desk and asked for my card. I was in the decorator design floor, covering business in a fairly exclusive area near B. Altman's. And on the adjacent corner was Maurice Villency/Roche Bobois decorator design interiors. She asked if she could send her husband in later in the afternoon as she saw some floor coverings that she liked. I let her know that we were open until six in the evening. And sure as all hell, at approximately five o'clock, in walked a young gentleman with my card in his hand. He asked for Chuck, and we exchanged pleasantries; so let's get into the nitty-gritty of luck of the Irish.

His name was Peter, about five-eight and about 150 pounds soaking wet. He told me what his wife had looked at and presented me with a list of carpet samples he would like to look at for the possibility of carpeting his brand-new one-bedroom condo at Fortieth Street and Lexington Avenue in New York City. In a few minutes, he got it all down pat, knew exactly what his wife picked out—great quality, expensive carpet in two different pastel shades. I asked him for a deposit after giving him a price. I don't remember exactly, but he did drop a thousand or two cash deposit on my desk and signed the order. I subsequently told him when I was available to measure the job and finalize the order in the next few days. We immediately became friends since he mentioned Thoroughbred racehorses. And in a heartbeat, we were both discussing great equine animals, owners, trainers, jockeys, and all the usual rhetoric that two horsemen would expand upon. Within a couple of days, we came together again, crossed the *t*'s and dotted the *i*'s, and we got his order to the starting gate. We had so much in common; it was kind of scary.

Over a number of meetings and drinks, I completed his order. And in conversation, he mentioned going to Lexington since he was anticipating selling his mare in foal later in November 1987 (which eventually happened, and I subsequently had written a story about that). Let's go to the spring of 1988, going to the races at Aqueduct that spring. Peter mentioned he had acquired a young horse by the name of Irish Blue Blood, and he was looking for a spot to run her in a claiming race at Aqueduct. One day—I believe it was in early May—he asked if I wanted to go to the races as his horse was entered in the fourth race the next day. It was midweek and I said, "No problem." He said he would pick me up around noon. The horse would be going to post in the fourth around two thirty, and we'd have lunch. We got to the track, give or take around 12:30 p.m. before the first race, had a quick bite, played a race or two, and his race was fast approaching. About twenty-five minutes prior to post time, we weaved our way and ambled down through the jockeys' room. Peter, knowing everyone, quickly, introduced me to a very short gentleman, cleaning some silks and preparing some riding boots for one of the jockeys riding in the race. His name was Luis Olah. Let me quickly mention Luis. He was, in 1988, a retired jockey, and for the most part, he was considered a valet for the jockey colony in New York. His official designation was *Keeper of the Silks*. I couldn't believe it, I bet on 4' 8" Luis Olah as a youngster when he was a grizzled veteran back in the early sixties. Luis was a New Yorker of Hungarian descent, born on the fourth of July in 1928. He was one of nine children, and broke his maiden, his first winner, in 1947. In the early sixties, I bet a thirty-five hundred claimer at Aqueduct by the name of Glenwood Road, ridden by a no-name jockey by the name of Luis Olah, honestly as a youngster in my late teens, not knowing all that much about the subtleties of the race game and studying the *Tele*, the predecessor of the *Daily Racing Form*. For some reason, I was drawn to this long shot. There was just something about him, an older five- or six-year-old who carried himself well, and looking up at the board, I didn't believe my eyes. He was 50–1. I put a deuce to win on him, and he came from the clouds, roaring home a two-length winner. Today, as I speak, I don't remember much other than his name and his rider. I can't attest as to who the trainer or barn was—all I know is that I collected $104 and change after the race was over.

As Peter and I then walked through the jockeys, saying hello to the likes of Angel Cordero, Jorge Velasquez, Bobby Ussery, Bill Boland, Johnny Ruane, and others, they were putting on their boots and their colors, getting ready to saddle up for the fourth race. We went through to the paddock area, where Irish Blue Blood was being saddled by Peter's trainer, Bruce Levine. After a few minutes, Peter went off to the opposite end of the walking circle to speak to some other owners and trainers, leaving me alone. Bruce asked me to hold the shank until he got back, then Bruce ambled off to see Peter. With about ten minutes to post, Randy Romero, a great rider, came over and introduced himself to me. And within minutes, the bugler called for riders up, and Randy asked me for a leg up. Being ambidextrous, I said "sure." I shifted the lead shank from my right hand to my left (just to the horse's left) and gave Randy a leg up. Not realizing it was so late, Bruce and Peter rushed back. Bruce, taking hold of the shank, led him out of his stall, handing the shank to the outrider, who led the horse onto the track in the post parade.

By the way, I don't know the exact date, but I can tell you a fact that Peter had asked me just a week prior if I wanted to buy in on a one-quarter share of Irish Blue Blood. I asked how much that was going to be, and he said it'd be $6,250. "Horse cost me twenty-five *g*'s." I said, "Let me think it over, and I'll let you know tomorrow." I said, "You know, I have quite a few horses in California." And he said, "Yes, I know. Just thought you might be interested."

The next day, I said "Peter, thanks, but I think I'll pass on her" as we were driving out to Aqueduct Racetrack to see her run. Here was the irony of it all. At about two thirty in the afternoon, the previously mentioned race was about ready to go off, and while at lunch with Peter, we discussed her chances of winning. He said, "I think she has a shot, but Oscar Barrera has a pretty good favorite in there. Everyone is betting him. He's been real hot of late. You know, anything he sends out on the track has been winning. Frankly, I can't remember the horse's name, but I know the horse was odds-on." Irish Blue Blood went off at a generous six to one, or so Peter and I put a double sawbuck each on her nose.

The bell rang, the gates opened, and they were on their way in a six-furlong event. Randy Romero broke well, put the horse mid pack in the 3–4 path with two horses inside of him, and on the far turn, he started to range up, picking up a horse or two. But old Oscar had his horse sitting second or third, moving up about to take the lead at the head of the stretch. At the eighth pole, Oscar had a clear four-length lead. Peter's horse came out of the pack, moved up smoothly, and challenged for second, and both horses pulled away from the field at the sixteenth pole. Oscar won by two or three lengths. Irish Blue Blood gallantly and clearly finished up some five or six lengths ahead of the field. Peter and I looked at each other, tore up our tickets, and said, "Oh well, she ran a good race."

Now here's the rub. Peter called me a few days later and told me that Oscar's horse tested positive for drugs. The rules of the game were such that everyone went home that day, and whoever bet Oscar's horse collected on their wager. Irish Blue Blood placed second and paid off for place and show, and the exotics such as exactas, quinellas, and trifectas all paid off as the final finish was exactly as it was. The only change was Oscar Barrera—because of his horse testing positive. The horse and the owner were not awarded the purse money, and the winning end of the purse was 60 percent of $32,000, which was $19,000 and change. And if I had taken him up on his offer to buy into 25 percent of Irish Blue Blood, my end of the purse would have been $4,800, give or take, after expenses of the race, such as a few points to the trainer and jockey and his fees.

So what we had was the good, the bad, and the ugly. Let's take the good: Peter's tickled he got the dough. The bad: Peter and I both lost some cash. But I am not the proud 25 percent owner of Irish Blue Blood. And if you ran the numbers, $6,250 and incorporate 25 percent of the purse ($4,800), I would have become the proud one-quarter partner for approximately $1,450. And the ugly was, Oscar Barrera, on May 17, 1988, drew a forty-five-day suspension from the stewards. In July, when he returned to training, everybody and his parakeet had their eyes on him. He had to be a picture-perfect gentleman and keep his nose clean. And he goes on a "zero for one hundred thirty" drought and doesn't have his next winner until January 1989. How 'bout dem apples.

So now we have my friend Peter and trainer Bruce Levine, who, in the past, trained not only Irish Blue Blood, the focus of this story, but also Peter's great filly, Lady on the Run, winner of five consecutive stakes races before she hurt herself, earning out at $255,000, and being retired when she took a bad step. Kudos to Bruce Levine, big hands-on trainer of many impressive Thoroughbreds such as the aforementioned Lady on the Run, Koluctoos Jill, Spring Beauty, Notchas Trace, Valid Wager, Coyote Lake, and the more recent Bustin Stones.

Oscar Barrera, younger brother of Hall-of-Fame trainer Laz Barrera, and trainer of Louis Wolfson's, Harbor View Farms' brilliant 1978 Triple Crown champion, Affirmed, ridden by a young Stevie Cauthen, finally started to have some winners in January of 1989. Once again— the good, the bad, the ugly.

For Pete's Sake! The Lady's on the Run! It's Her Big 40!

For lack of originality and possibly better judgment, I attempt to address this tale. You may just be reading my last words. I may, or should I say, certainly will be shot, especially if I attempt to follow my Polish path. You may ask the question. I will answer, so go ahead; oh, the question, if you cannot figure this no-brainer, you're in worse shape than me. The Polish path is exactly that, attempting to do exactly what you know your wife will kill you over. With that, I foolishly proceed.

Big day—November 8, 1987—you guessed it, Big 40. Hers, not mine. This is going to be a saga, so please bear with me. Remember, I know no other way. Please, dear God, let me survive this test.

Let the fun begin! I will unfold the conglomeration by first making the necessary introductions. As I remember, oh so clearly, almost a week after her birthday and no party, at Kennedy Airport, at a small round table in the lounge, seated to my immediate right was my wife. Ten minutes later, my friend Peter sauntered up, followed by his wife, Valerie. Peter saw me, extended his hand, and we made introductions. Oh, I forgot one little detail—we were headed for Louisville, Kentucky. We ordered a round of drinks, boarded the plane, and off we went. This brilliant plan was because my wife didn't like parties. Peter and I did a little business together. I sold him and Valerie carpet for their new apartment. He and I hit it off from the get-go. We both had common ground—Thoroughbreds. He was selling his mare in foal in Keeneland's Fasig-Tipton sales. I asked if he and his wife wanted company, and the adventure was born. We flew to Kentucky and could not stop conversing on the flight. It was over much too quickly. By the way, it was the first time the wives had ever met—scary—but fear not, everything worked out to a fare thee well. We picked up our town car upon arrival and sped off to the Lexington Grand Hyatt.

We ate, ran off to Keeneland Racetrack, and checked the mare at 10:00 p.m. Peter noticed she was circling her stall, which only meant that she'd been up all day and that she created a lot of interest in her. We calmed her down and waited a while until she settled in for the evening. On the return to the Hyatt, Peter said she should command a hefty price. After all, her breeding was impeccable. She was by *Bailjumper*, a stakes-winning turf horse beyond belief out of the mare *Young and Foolish*, and her granddaddy was the great Greentree Stable stallion *Tom Fool*. Kudos to the owners in naming her *Lady on the Run*. Are you kidding? So apropos.

Peter, on the prowl to claim a good one, had his eyes on this three-year-old filly who hadn't run until her three-year-old campaign. Her first two tries were in maiden special weight races. She wasn't for sale, then the owner gave up on her and dropped her into a $20,000 claimer at the Meadowlands. Peter pulled off a great claim and he is now the proud owner of the filly. We had a 7:00 a.m. wake-up call. We were all exhausted and said good night. The next morning, we all went back for the early morning sale. Incredibly, it started at 9:00 a.m. Peter was hip no. 580. Much too early, no one was in the pavilion, no one! We were in a world of trouble. Let's relax, we need a great and imaginative plan. A piece of cake. Please let me interject and convey a thought about another friend, Don Boccio, who once said, "God forgive them for they know not what they do." We needed to act quickly. It was us against the system and the good ole boys in Kentucky, and it was all about dollars. At 9:00 a.m. sharp, the auctioneer took the podium. At approximately 9:20 a.m., we were going to be the eighth horse to be auctioned. I'll say this, I believe we were successful in our attempt to maximize the situation. Back to the plan, we realized no one knew we were in town from New York; a plus. After all, the good ole boys were slick. We won't let them steal her. In less than thirty minutes, we had it under control.

Let me take you back to the early morning and preface what I've just said. Peter's trainer, Bruce Levine, Glencrest Farms, advised him of a $100,000 offer for his mare. In good faith, Bruce advised Peter of a substantial offer for his mare and asked if he wanted to pull her from the sale. The answer was an emphatic, "No, sorry, but I'll take my chances." Let me explain. I will address a complex and interesting reason. Simply and to the point, *Lady on the Run* won five consecutive New York Stakes races, earning $255K; it was huge, considering females earn one-third of their male counterparts. Peter's trainer, Bruce Levine, guided the filly to all her smashing wins. If she had not taken a bad step in training in late 1986, she would have continued on. But obviously, for every bit of good luck, there was also bad luck that came along with it. Bruce advised Peter that she was too valuable to go on and take a chance on breaking down. So the advice was, through his connections at Glencrest Farms in Kentucky, let's breed her to their standing stallion *Sport'n Life*. A Northern Dancer, infamous as the horse who left Del Carroll lifeless on the track in the early morning while training. In early '87, after the *Lady* was put in foal in February to *Sport'n Life*, *Alysheba* won the Kentucky Derby on the first Saturday in May and followed up with a great victory in the Preakness two weeks later and was in line for a shot at the 1987 Triple Crown. Subsequently, three weeks later, *Alysheba* went off the odds-on favorite in the Belmont. There was, on Belmont day, approaching the finish line, silence. *Bet Twice* upsets *Alysheba*, and the glory of a Triple Crown is over. This catapulted *Sport'n Life's* sire value, since *Sport'n Life* was the sire of *Bet Twice*. The breeding fee increased from $16K to $60K instantaneously. Now you can understand why Peter said no. The *Lady* was the earliest of eleven covers in the sale. This meant she was impregnated in February; the other ten were later in the season, and her foal would be the most mature animal to be born from the sale. This made her the most valuable commodity of the group, and if someone offered $100K, Peter was right to say no to the private sale.

Peter took the supreme gamble and decided to go to auction. The handler brought the mare before the auctioneer. She was all dolled up, dappled, and looked great. We crossed our fingers and hoped she demanded a big price. Peter had moved about a dozen seats to my right. I was in the center of the pavilion, Marion and Valerie about a dozen seats to my left. Only two other bidders were in the pavilion, one to the upper and far left, another to the upper and far right. The auctioneer started the bidding. He said, "Do I hear $50K, $50K, $50K, $50K?" Silence. He said it again, and he repeated himself a third time. Still silence. He then began his rhetoric, "Come on, guys, she's beautiful. Look at the breeding. Let's have a bid here." Still silence. He dropped to $25K and started all over again at the reduced level. These two other individuals were salivating, just waiting for the auctioneer to reduce it again, and one of them was about to steal her. Just before the auctioneer was about to reduce the price again, Peter threw his hand in the air; a thumb and four fingers waved vigorously. The auctioneer accepted the bid at $25K. Now he asked, "Do I hear $50K?" He repeated himself a half dozen times. Silence.

Suddenly, another guy threw his hand up the same way.

"I've got 50, 50, 50. Do I hear 75, 75, 75?" No other takers. Before the hammer came down, Peter raised his hand again and outbid the guy. Bid accepted. The auctioneer asked, "Do I hear 100, 100, 100?"

The new rival went to $100K. Peter went to $125K. He was countered by $150K, still not a whisper. This was getting scary and old. Suddenly, the other bidder joined the bidding. The bidding continued and came to an end minutes later, and Peter walked away with a handsome sum.

Peter said, "Let's go. I have to go to the sales window, sign papers, and get the check." Peter returned with check in hand. Waving it, he laughed and said, "Let's go eat and party."

We all headed back to the Grand Hyatt. We won, if you could call it that.

When we got to the hotel mid to late afternoon, Peter went to the dining room to make a reservation for dinner. He joined us back in the lounge and ordered a bottle of Tattinger's Reserve at ninety dollars a bottle. We enjoyed the afternoon and waited for the call for dinner. A couple of bottles and a couple of hours later, we were called to dinner. At this impressive restaurant, Peter ordered another bottle to toast Marion's birthday. Kudos to everyone. Great morning, afternoon, and evening. Peter and I wandered off to the shoeshine lady, dressed in a tux. We sat in the two high chairs. She handed us a cigar each. Peter was first, me second, and thirty minutes later, we were done. Peter dropped a Ulysses S. Grant on her. We were enjoying the hell out of ourselves and walked back to join the ladies at the table. It was about 9:00 p.m., and Peter said, "We are done."

We said, "Yes."

Peter got the bill and would not let me go in my pocket. "We're in my territory," he explained. He took a gander at the bill, put six or seven Franklins on the table, and said, "Let's get the hell out of here, and let's go dancing."

Without further ado, we woke up Sunday for the hourlong drive back to Louisville. We had a few hours to kill before the flight back. Peter, not knowing what to do and having never been in Kentucky, said, "What do you want to do?" I had no problem. I looked at Marion in the backseat. With a smile, I said, "Hey, Peter, perfect. Let's catch a couple at Churchill."

He instantly said, "Good idea, never been there."

We left a couple of hours later, short a few bucks; we caught the plane and took off and said good-bye to my old Kentucky home.

Real Inside Info

Truthfully, I can actually only remember two times when I actually had what I would consider real inside information on any Thoroughbred. Truth be told, I could've had some information that would be considered inside information other than these two times, but I won't speak of those situations only because it may be considered embellishment. The first time was in the early summer of 1987, when I had my floor-covering showroom at 200 Madison Avenue at Thirty-Sixth Street, New York City. We had a foal that spring, a filly that had to be named. Since the Jockey Club was located at 380 Madison Avenue near Forty-Eighth Street, I decided to take a walk during the lunch hour and I had my trusty list of names with me. You see, when naming any Thoroughbred, you must list five names from one to five, number 1 being your first choice and so on. When naming them at that time, the name could not have been used nationally or internationally in the past twenty-five years, or for that matter, any great name such as Man O' War or Secretariat can never be used again. On the top of my list was Double Royalty. Everyone has a preference in how they decide on naming their animals. Mine was to take something from the mare and something from the stallion and be creative. Since the mare's name was Gold Queen and the stallion was named Damascus Prince, we had a queen and a prince in the name, so it was very obvious that this was a slam dunk. We have royalty in both their veins, so now you have Double Royalty.

As I approached the Jockey Club, which was located on one of the umpteenth floors of that skyscraper, I entered this very posh outer office, was greeted, asked about my business there, and I said I wanted to name a filly. I was told to take a seat and someone would be with me shortly. Sitting in the same area was a slightly older lady, and if I were to take a guess, in her fifties, She was very well-dressed in a business suit. We sat around for some twenty to thirty minutes, exchanged pleasantries, and she was there for the same purpose.

My partner and I were entertaining thoughts and had an attorney working on putting together a syndication on a three-year-old we owned by the name of Artistic, sired by Sanhedrin who ran third to Seattle Slew and Run Dusty Run in the 1977 Belmont. The lady seemed interested and asked me for my card. The amount for a share in Artistic was extremely small in comparison to today's mega bucks. She said her driver was waiting down on Madison Avenue and she would be in touch with me as she had to fly back to Minneapolis that afternoon. She took care of her business, and as she left, she said, "You will be hearing from me." A few minutes later, I did the same.

A few weeks later, I was surprised she called. She told me that they were racing some of their horses at Canterbury Downs. Her husband, a doctor, was interested in the figures and the breeding that I afforded her. She asked if her vet, who knew another vet in Southern California, could check the horse out. Through our tête-à-tête over the next month, playing phone tag, I learned that she had a three-year-old in New York in Michael Hushion's barn at Aqueduct. In a letter she sent, thanking me but turning us down on Artistic, she mentioned that she had a little bad luck with her three-year-old in New York. The horse caught a quarter crack and came up a little gimpy. The only thing I can remember today was the horse was a sprinter by Lt. Stevens.

Another couple of weeks go by, and as my usual MO, I checked the entries every day in the *Daily News*. I saw her horse entered. I believe it was the fifth or sixth race, only seven entries. Her horse was even money; Fat Frank, a horse I had been looking out for was entered and was the 3–1 second choice. The other five horses on the morning line were 5–1, 6–1, 8–1, 15 and 21–1. I decided to go to the track. When the race came up, I had an ulterior motive to see how her horse came up in the saddling area and in the post parade, and see how the betting went. Since she'd told me just a couple of weeks earlier that her horse had problems and didn't look all that great on the track, I decided to throw the filly out of the race; let everybody else go down the tubes at 4–5 when betting closed, while Fat Frank went down to 5–2 and the next three horses were 7–1, 8–1, and 10–1, and the other two were betting off at well over 20–1 each. So I made a stand, I bet Fat Frank in an exacta with the three other horses, twenty-dollar straight exactas. Her horse broke quickly, got on the lead, and halfway down the backstretch, started falling back as Fat Frank started pulling away into the turn by three or four lengths. My other three horses, the 7, 8, and 10–1 shots were running second, third, and fourth. Wow, the two long shots in the race quickly gobbled up her 4–5 shot and the race was history. Her horse ran dead last. Fat Frank, 5–2, the second horse 7–1 in a seven-horse field with the favorite out. I was hoping to pay sixty or seventy dollars for the exacta. When the board lit up, it was only forty-one dollars, but I did have it ten times collecting over $410 on a twenty-dollar bet.

The only other time that I truly remember having inside information was in 1991. We owned and ran Pacific Coast Stables. I was there with my buddy Jimmy, my wife was in New York, and we had a client by the name of Johnny Longden, famous jockey and one of the leading riders of all time. He brought a horse to us at Pacific Coast Stables, a two-year-old by Eleven Stitches. We at Pacific Coast Stables were situated on fifteen acres, that's to say two-and-a-half acres by approximately seven acres. The track was five-eighths of a mile, starting out of a chute near the front of the property, and the main body was just short of a one-half oval, very similar to a harness track and fairly narrow with sharp turns. We had a three-stall starting gate out of the chute and three eight-stall barns, twenty-four twelve-by-twelve corrals and two one-half acre pens, two hot walkers, and a $100,000 hydro treadmill, state of the art. Johnny and his agent/caregiver would drive up every Saturday at approximately ten o'clock in the morning to watch his horse workout. Our training track was basically for lay-ups, galloping horses coming off the track or going to the track. On a daily basis, the exercise riders would just gallop them; a two-minute lick at best. One Saturday, Juan tacked up Johnny's two-year-old, walked him out of the barn, and I heard Johnny telling the boy, "I want to see you breeze the horse three furlongs." Juan said, "We don't breeze them here, we only gallop them here." Johnny said sternly, "Breeze her. I want to see what she's got." Juan got a leg up, went on to the track, and galloped her clockwise before he started the workout.

My friend Jim came up and I told him that Johnny told Juan to breeze her three. Jim said, "He's not going to breeze her. Don't worry, he's not going to breeze her. He knows better." We had inside and outside gooseneck rail around the track, walking up to the rail approaching Johnny to see his filly, Juan turned the horse around and started to gallop. He got her in stride and hit the three-eighths marker, and the filly picked it up, approached the turn, and Jim and I couldn't believe our eyes. We said, "Johnny, what are you doing?"

He didn't have an answer and he walked away. Juan brought the filly in, all hot and lathered. We unsaddled her, sprayed her down with water in front of the barn, walked her around the barn a couple of times, and ten minutes later, we had her on the hot walker. Johnny and his guy hung around for the next half hour to forty-five minutes, and I got Johnny on the side and I said, "Johnny, what are you doing with that horse? You know you shouldn't be breezing this horse here. You're going to break her down." I then said, "Johnny, there's always tomorrow. You've got a long time with this, baby."

His answer to me was, "When you're eighty-four, there aren't many tomorrows."

Both he and his caregiver left at about 11:30 a.m. Jimmy left to go to his girlfriend Jean's house at about 2:00 p.m. A few minutes later, I decided to go back to the barn area and see how Johnny's two-year-old was doing. I checked the fronts and there was heat in both knees, cannon bone, and I knew it was over. I called to let him know and he said, "Don't worry about it. I know what I'm doing." Within three or four days, somebody came by and said Johnny wanted me to pick up the filly. Everything was in order and off they went. I took it he didn't like what I said.

About two months later, Jim and I were at the local off-track betting parlor in San Bernardino, and on the card in a maiden race, his horse was entered in a six-furlong event as the 2–1 favorite in a twelve-horse field. Jim and I looked at each other. In California, the name Longden attracted enormous attention. Jim and I were playing the ponies with about ten or twenty acquaintances, and we told them we had the horse at our track. They said the horse would win off easy. We said, "We'll book your bets." They laughed at us. We bet the second choice in the race at about 3 or 4–1. Johnny's horse went off at even money. The acquaintances said we were crazy, and Johnny's horse couldn't lose. We said the horse would not even hit the board, and they collectively gave us about 10–1 and I said, "I'll bet you another twenty dollars that the horse runs dead last." I wished I had the chart that day. I reluctantly accepted 100–1 on the twenty. You can check the chart. Not only did he run last, but the chart also read DNF: the horse did not finish the race, never crossed the finish line. I collected $400 or $500; it took me weeks to collect and I never got the rest. If that's not inside information, I don't know what is.

1992 Chuck, Jim and Hall of Fame jockey and trainer Johnny Longden. Training Track Winchester, Ca. Johnny retired in 1966 at 59. His 6,032 wins by far the most of any jockey.

Fools Galore

The second and only other trip I took to the Jockey Club was again early summer '89 to name another homebred; this time, a colt. As the story goes, the colt was a son of the California-bred *Looks Impressive* out of our mare *Greek Sweetie*. The previous year, when we were looking for a stallion to breed to *Greek Sweetie*, we sat down with a breeder and listened to his stories. We saw his stallion *Looks Impressive*. He was by stakes winner *Lucky Mel*, and we were considering him. *Lucky Mel* was by Olympia out of a mare by the *Pie King*; the credentials seemed reasonable. We made a final commitment and bred *Greek Sweetie*. This decision was made after we were told a story about *Looks Impressive*. *Looks Impressive* raced as a three- and four-year-old of 1974 and 1975 and had twelve starts, winning four and finishing third twice. In his tenth and eleventh start, he won an allowance race, followed up with nonwinners of two in his eleventh start, and also won that one before his twelfth and final start. An offer came in for the son of *Lucky Mel* for $75,000. The horse had four wins, two thirds in eleven starts, and now they were attempting to run seven and a half furlongs on the turf at Santa Anita. The owner and prospective buyer were trying to make a deal prior to the race. Things got a little testy, and both walked away from the table with no deal. Five days later, the race was run at Santa Anita. The strange thing about the configuration of the seven-and-a-half furlong strip was that it started out on the grass, and as they made the turn at the top of the stretch, it crossed the main track for about twenty to thirty yards and back onto the grass.

That day, *Looks Impressive*, we were told, was running well, looking like he could be a winner, came off the grass, hit the main track, and broke down. That's when one fool had offered $75,000 for the horse and the second fool refused the offer.

We go on to name our colt, and since he's by *Looks Impressive* out of *Greek Sweetie*, a Greek Money mare who ran in the 1962 Kentucky Derby, our top name was *Looksgreektome*. Funny thing, 1991 rolled around and he was a two-year-old. Marion and I were in New York, not in California, and we heard of a horse doing great things by the name of *Itsallgreektome*. We thought we had a big horse. We jumped for joy, thinking we had a good thing; and before our feet hit the ground, we realized *Itsallgreektome* was not our colt.

So considering *Looksgreektome* ran twice in his lifetime, never hitting the board, although going off as the favorite in his last try. So between the two fools mentioned above and fools like us who listen to the story, we went home empty.

A New Era

Before the end of the eighties came about, I felt it necessary to reflect back on a previous story I've written concerning the Fasig-Tipton yearling sales of the early 1980s, when my wife and myself went to Saratoga, just the two of us, and became more heavily involved with the sales. As I've stated before, it was really something to experience like Carly Simon sang in her song "He's so vain, this song is about him. / He's so vain, he goes to Saratoga and his horse naturally won. / He flies off to Nova Scotia to see a total eclipse of the sun." The grandeur of it all was truly amazing, to be at this venue and sale in August. What more can a real horseman, or for that matter, anyone experiencing these beautiful and talented equine specimens ask for?

All this brings me to our next subject. Both my wife and myself were having dinner at the Marriott Renaissance in town in the early evening the night of the sales, having a glass of wine with dinner, when some hubbub drew our attention to the entrance of the dining room. That evening, Sheikh Mohammed bin Rashid Al Maktoum appeared in full traditional garb with his entourage. We found out later in the evening that this group of approximately thirty people was royally attended to, and word got out at dinner that they were occupying the seventh floor of the hotel. As stated before, in that period of time, when the foreigners did plunder some of our greatest bloodlines in America since the dollar was cheap in relation to foreign currencies, we were not aware of the master plan at work; now, in retrospect, I can speak of it. Connecting all the dots, it made sense that the fact that Sheikh Mohammed bin Rashid Al Maktoum, being the avid horseman that he was, had a vision. His affinity and burning desire was to attract major Thoroughbred horse racing to the Arabian Peninsula in Dubai. Along with that and his never-ending profits from the oil industry, another vision he had was to build a racecourse and replicate Churchill Downs. He accomplished that and also attracted many of the greatest Thoroughbreds of the era. His efforts seemed incredibly rewarding. In history, the Thoroughbred racehorses were direct disciples of the great black Arabian stallions; but his never-ending thirst to win the greatest treasure in all of racing, the Kentucky Derby, eluded him.

From what I understand and believe, the fact is that he, his buyers, and/or agents continue to comb the world today for the best stallions, brood mares, and Thoroughbreds in training. Thirty years later, absolutely older and presumably wiser, his thirst still abounds in an effort to climb that mountain and reach the pinnacle at all costs.

The Mirage Thoroughbred Handicapper's Challenge

In the early part of 1991, my friend Jimmy came out from Houston to live at Pacific Coast Stables, my fifteen-acre training track in Winchester, California. He had just had a heart attack, and I told him he could pick up some pocket money while recuperating at the track. He did so. I usually came out a few times a year, spending four-day weekends and checking to see how things were going.

In June, I came out and found that I had to stay for an extended period of time because of business. Around the Fourth of July weekend that year, after taking care of all our duties, harrowing the training track and preparing it for the morning workouts, we decided to spend a day at the races. When we got to the track, picking up the forms, we saw a full-page advertisement for the Mirage Hotel's First Annual Thoroughbred Handicapper's tournament. It stated the tournament would be held at the new Mirage Hotel on Thursday, July 25, and Friday, July 26. Entries must be paid for in full, no later than Wednesday afternoon, July 24. It sounded interesting. Normally, we would trash our papers, programs, and losing tickets, and go back to the ranch. But that day, we kept one racing form and brought it back to the ranch. Since I had some problems at the ranch that necessitated my staying beyond my three- or four-day weekend, we decided to toss around the idea that if I should have to stay any length of time, we would consider entering the tournament together.

By the middle of the month, we started to seriously consider going to the tournament. We had one dilemma—we had just committed earlier in the year to take over ownership of a three-year-old filly who was being prepared and had actually run a few races. As it turned out, this filly wasn't exactly a world-beater, as a matter of fact, she was basically a $20,000–$25,000 claimer. She'd bucked her shins as a two-year-old and had been on the sidelines for about six months. She was pin fired, recouped, and had a few races in her, and our trainer was looking for a spot to race her. The one good caveat was her breeding. She was a daughter of Breeders' Cup classic winner Skywalker, winner of the Third Breeders' Cup classic! She was out of a mare by the name of Sunset Hour, who was by the sire Tumiga. So she was pretty well bred and somewhat correct. Looking for a spot to race her, and with the tournament coming up, ironically, a spot opened in the conditions book, and she was set to be entered on Friday, the twenty-sixth. Decision time! Tournament or racetrack? We analyzed everything and made a decision to go to Las Vegas and enter the tournament and pass up the opportunity to take a photo.

Quite a dilemma, and let me give you the reasons. We probably would have bet five hundred, maybe a thousand, to win on her at Del Mar, since she would probably be 5–1 or 6–1, and our trainer found an easy spot for her. And she had a somewhat reasonable chance of winning. It was still a gamble; but should we win, we could possibly pick up three or four thousand.

Now let me tell you the parameters of the tournament. Two guys from Brooklyn put their heads together and came up with a theory. The entry fee of the tournament was $1,000, kind of a push betting our horse at Del Mar, and picking up three or four thousand should the horse win or the same thousand-dollar entry fee, but $350,000 in prize money put up by the Mirage Hotel. No-brainer!

There were perks in the tournament. The $1,000 entry fee into the tournament bought you one entry, hotel accommodations for you and your wife, girlfriend, or partner, and three nights—Wednesday, Thursday, and Friday on the cuff. The Wednesday welcome reception party in the grand ballroom had all the bells and whistles, outrageous gourmet delights, seafood, filet mignon, prime rib, and all the trimmings, along with any and all beverages. Eagle-eye Jimmy said, "Look to the left of the dessert table." As the masses went to the beef and fish, Jimmy and I made a quick left, heads bobbing, and we ended in a photo finish just a few inches from the dark chocolate topped with fresh raspberries and cream, which we attacked with a vengeance. The guest speakers were Harvey Pack, race commentator of the show *Pack at the Track*; tournament director Steve Wolfson, son of Louis Wolfson, owner of Affirmed and Harbor View Farms; and Steve Wynn, CEO and owner of the Mirage Hotel. Then there was the great jockey Jerry Bailey and trainer Frankie Brothers, Kentucky Derby trainer of Hansel, who finished tenth to winner *Strike the Gold,* eventually winning the Preakness and Belmont, ridden to victory by Jerry Bailey. For the two days of the tournament, Thursday and Friday, there was free flowing booze and a huge all-you-can-eat luncheon buffet for the day. Starting from the first race of the day on the East Coast at approximately 10:00 a.m., the races at Saratoga and Gulfstream, midcountry at Arlington Park, and winding up with the later cards at Del Mar and Golden Gate Fields, and the coup de grace, formal dinner and awards ceremonies along with, of course, all the gelt. Let me simply break down the gelt, $350,000, $300,000 to the winner of the tournament, and the other $50,000 being split up in two other ways. Let's count the ways: $25,000 split between the top five individuals with the most winners over two days, $5,000 awarded to the winners of each racetrack was broken up $3,000 for first, $1,000 for second, $500 for third, and $250 for fourth and fifth. Considering the alternatives, these two Brooklyn guys felt strongly that we could put our heads together and try to win either the most winners or at least one of the tracks and at least get our money back and have a field day with all the perks. Should we get super lucky, we could win it all. The cost to the Mirage—three hundred and fifty rooms at $140 per night for three nights—was $1, 470, 000. The cost of the grand ballroom for four days was $470,000. Food and drink for approximately five hundred people was another $200,000. It must have cost the Mirage $2 million to try and get this tournament off the ground for its maiden voyage. So as far as we were concerned, it was a total win-win experience.

Tournament Part Two—Yaw

After checking in and getting our fabulous room, I took the first queen size bed and Jimmy got stuck near the air conditioner closer to the window with his bed. I did that purposely because he snored, hoping the air conditioner would drown out the noise. It didn't matter, as things turned out, because we didn't get to sleep until 4:00 a.m., handicapping five racetracks, nine races on each card, forty-five races in all, and discussing speed figures until we were bleary-eyed.

While handicapping, a number of things jumped off the paper at me. The first day the fourth race at Saratoga was a steeplechase race. Jokingly, having total recall, I told Jimmy this horse Yaw couldn't lose. He was a mortal lock. I said, "This will be our major bet of the tournament." He looked at me as if I was crazy and said, "Have you lost your mind?"

He looked at the racing form and said, "The last time that horse ran, he ran at MAL [short for Malvern racecourse], a 2 and ¼ mile nonbetting, steeplechase event at Radnor Hunt Club in Malvern, Pennsylvania, just outside of Philly, and ran fifth by thirteen in a five-horse field, and the race before that, ran at another country track and dumped the rider over the first hedge, and so you're insane."

I said, "No, listen, this horse can't lose."

He said, "They're going at Saratoga, there are nine horses in the field, there are two entries and seven betting interests, and he's the rank outsider at 15-1, and there isn't another horse at double-digit odds. That's what makes it so incredible. Let me tell you what I saw this horse do. This horse ran a race maybe a year or two ago, I can't remember exactly, but I saw with my own two eyes."

He looked at me again. "I don't care. This horse can't win. I'm calling a doctor. You really lost it."

I insisted and I said, "Just listen, this horse ran in a big race at Belmont. The horse went off at nice odds and he's by Seattle Slew. He's out of a really good grass broodmare by Luthier."

Jimmy said, "This horse is a nine-year-old."

I shook my head. "It doesn't matter. You have to see this horse go over the hedges. He's pure speed and can run all day long. The race I saw him run was utterly amazing. The horse was going two miles in change, and he immediately got on the lead. They came by the grandstand, the first time opened up a five-length lead, he went over the first jump and into the first turn, opened up the lead by about eight lengths, and then suddenly ducked to the inside, left the course, cut the cone, and within a fifth of a second, was back on the course. His rider went on with the horse, opening up a fifteen- to twenty-length lead, and he went on to win the race, romping to a win and breaking the track record. Before they got back to unsaddle, the inquiry sign went up. They disqualified him and placed him last. So now I ask you this. Do you think the horse has a chance?"

He said, "Where is the race? I don't see it on the past performance."

"Are you for real?" I replied, the famous last words to him. "Trust me, this horse is owned by Timber Bay Farm and trained by Jonathan Sheppard, big time, and has been a multiple winner at Saratoga. They're lurking in the bushes."

Bright and early the next morning, the tournament started with the first East Coast races at 1:00 p.m., 10:00 a.m. Vegas time. We just finished breakfast about 9:00 a.m. and we entered the grand ballroom at the Mirage. People moved everywhere, positioned themselves at tables, and got ready for the tournament. This first inaugural tournament drew professional handicappers, trainers, owners, and real hard-line horsemen for the most part. Jimmy and I went over to Steve Wolfson, who was standing and speaking with the above-mentioned celebrities, and we asked Steve where we should go. He directed us to a table with a few other people that he had been in contact with. In conversation with everybody gathered there, discussing horses that might be useful in getting ahead early in the tournament, Steve asked, "Do you have any good ideas?" Jimmy looked at me and said, "Go ahead, tell him." So I opened my mouth and out came, "Yaw, a mortal lock." They all looked at me with questions in their eyes. Somebody laughed and said, "Isn't that the steeplechase race at Saratoga?" And I said, "You got it." They all laughed. I went on to take ten minutes to meticulously give them every reason to play this equine diamond in the rough. Frankly, I honestly believed that these experts did not take heed, and approximately two hours later, the race went off, Yaw came romping home, and two strides from the wire under one stroke with a right hand whip on his flank, Jonathan Smart stuck his neck in front, paying thirty dollars even to win. The end of the tournament came on Saturday, along with the fabulous white-gloved awards dinner. After dinner, the master of ceremonies and director of the tournament, Steve Wolfson, came to the microphone and began the commencement of the awards. He started with the minor awards, even though in the thousands at each individual track, somewhere along the route, he finally got to Saratoga. Jimmy and I looked at each other. Here we go; where did we finish? We figured probably second or third. Steve, at the mic, called in ascending order the fiftht prize winner. As he called the name, we looked at each other and it wasn't us; he quickly called number four and once again, not us. Jimmy and I, with smiles on our faces, knew number three was coming up. We believed that at least finishing third, we would pick up a grand and at least break even for the tournament.

He called out the name; not us again. Now we began to wonder if we must be second. We held our breaths, waiting for our names to be blurted out by Steve. He said the second placer, called out the name, and it was someone else. We looked at each other a little pale in the face—is it possible we were shut out? It couldn't be. Now a little nervous, Steve Wolfson became very dramatic and started a dissertation. "Okay, folks, now this is going to be hard to believe, but the winner of the Saratoga event . . . but before I mention names, you're not going to believe this story. About an hour or two before the tournament began, Harvey Pack, myself, Jerry Bailey, Frankie Brothers, and Mirage Hotel owner Steve Wynn were in conversation with two guys from New York. They gave us a horse, a steeplechase horse at that, and called him a mortal lock. Unbelievable! As you guessed it, Jimmy and I were already celebrating, and as Steve called out our names as the winners of the Saratoga event, he said, "Give them a big hand and come up to receive your award." We won the top prize of $3,000 for Saratoga, and no one believed we could win on a steeplechase race. And for the rest of the tournament, we were like rock stars.

We spent $1,000, and we were wined, dined, and treated like royalty. We left Vegas and went back to California, trippling our investment.

Jonathan Smart Jockey aboard Yaw, their winning performance in steeplechase race July 1991 at Saratoga. Yaw's past performance and charts of his winning race with Jonathan aboard on following page.

4th Saratoga

2 1-16 MILES (Steeplechase)

Yew

b. g. 9, by Seattle Slew (Bold Reasoning) out of La Vire (Luthier)

148

Sar
Saratoga
July 25 1991
4s Hcp45000

TWO MILES AND ONE SIXTEENTH OVER NATIONAL FENCES. HANDICAP. Purse $45,000. Steeplechase. For Four Year Olds and Upward which have not won $27,000 twice in 1991. Weights Saturday, July 20. Declarations by 10:00 A.M., Monday, July 22.

Value of Race: $45,000 Winner: $27,000; 2nd: $9,900; 3rd: $5,400; 4th: $2,700

Last Raced	Horse	A	Wt	M/Eq	Jockey	Odds	PP	1	2	3	8	11	Fin	Comments
10May91 2Med⁶	Yew	9	143		J Smart	14.60	6							Well placed throughout, won drive
16Jun91 6Pim⁴	Mihenzi	6	144		G Alrock	12.60	5							Moved up with approaching 2nd turn
16Jun91 6Pim⁴	Three Bells For Me	7	135		V Schloway	10.60	3							Well placed, weakened
27Jun91 3Mtf⁷	Lights And Music	7	140		J Lawrence	10.70	1							Inside last turn, no rally
27Jun91 3Mtf¹	Skorpeo	9	142		J Tuter	5.50	1							Saved ground
8Jun91 4Bel⁴	Woody Boy Would	4	152		J Fisher	2.30	7							Led from start
4May91 5DeM⁴	Perascal	9	147		R Beggan	1.20	4							Dropped back
7Aug90 6Sar⁴	Peer Prince	6	134		PB Walsh	10.60	2							Well placed
6Jun91 4Bel⁷	Mede Noble	6	148		B Miller	1.20	8							Lost rider

#	Horse	$2 Mutuel Prices		
7	Yew	32.60	15.20	10.60
5	Mihenzi		12.60	7.20
A	Three Bells For Me			7.60

$2 Exacta (7-5) $341.60
$2 Quinella (5-7) $144.00

Time: 3:45.30
Won: Driving
Course: Firm
Off: 2:20pm

Yew, 1982 (Mar), gelding, b/by, by Seattle Slew (Bold Reasoning) out of La Vire (Luthier). Bred in KY by W. R. Hawn.

Mutuel Pool (W-P-S): $149,100. Exacta: $235,947. Quinella: $71,543. Total Wagering: $456,590.

Chuck and Jonathan February 2016, 25 years later meet
at the Steeplechase Museum in Camden, SC

August 2016 Marion and Jonathan Sheppard – Hall of
Fame trainer of steeplechase winner Yaw at Saratoga

Barn area at Saratoga August, 2016. Jonathan Sheppard winningest steeplechase trainer of all time at work.

The Board at Aqueduct

It was January '94. Jimmy and I received the mail at Pacific Coast Stables, our training track. In the mail, there was an invitation to go to the handicap tournament at Cal Neva in Reno, Nevada. After harrowing and prepping the racetrack very early Tuesday before daylight and previously telling our farm manager and trainer, Juan Vasquez, that we were going to Reno for a few days for some business, and that weshould be back Saturday or Sunday, and you can reach us on Jimmy's pager if there's any problem. God only knows how we went up there. It was about 550 to 600 miles, taking the back highways and byways, Route 66, and others heading north. When we left the ranch in Hemet, California, it was comfortable in the seventies. We didn't bring much heavy winter clothing—wrong move. It was about a ten-hour trip, but we lollygagged along since we didn't know what we were in for, not realizing we were traveling north into the ski area in the Sierra Nevadas in the area of Yosemite National Park. As we were going up, we began climbing up the snaky plowed road that was still icy with snowdrifts up to five to six feet. The majestic mountains were fully snow clad. When we finally plateaued, we started moving across the area past the exit for Lake Tahoe to our left and followed the signs to Reno.

When we got to Reno, we checked into a local hotel casino since the Cal Neva was only a casino, not a hotel. We immediately went over to register for the tournament. This tournament was incredible. Unlike the handicapper's challenge at the Mirage in Las Vegas, it was only $500 (not $1,000) to enter. And it wasn't a pure entry fee. It was a $500 account, and you had ten bets every day. But when you won, it was either deducted or added to your account; and whatever your final account balance was after the three days of the tournament, you would walk away with whatever was in the account. The idea was to be high on the list of winners as $50,000 was the ultimate prize, and $30,000 went to the top winner as a prize, excluding your winners or losers in your private account. Albeit, in the handicapper's challenge, $350,000 was based on a $1,000 entry fee times 350 entrants—zero put up by the casino. And if you didn't win, you lost a grand. In the tournament, the entry fee could come back to you in spades; and the casino actually put up the $50,000 in prizes to attract the clients.

We quickly learned the ropes. The Cal Neva not only put up $50,000 in prizes but also gave you carte blanche for virtually breakfast, lunch, and dinner. You see, they had two restaurants. We found they had lunch at both restaurants between 11:00 a.m. and 1:00 p.m. and dinner after 5:00 p.m. We went to the early sitting at the main-level restaurant on the first day before the tournament started, when we signed up, and they had the special for the handicappers. Since it was an open casino, all you had to do was show your credentials and eat for free. The waiter approached and told us the menu. You get all the typical hot and cold lunches or the special. When he reeled off the specials, our eyes opened. Never tell two guys from Brooklyn about the specials. The specials were a six-ounce filet mignon along with two slipper lobster tails with drawn butter. Or if you desired no beef, you could have three slipper lobster tails with all the trimmings. Jimmy and I looked at each other. It was a no-brainer; we would have the lobster tails. We didn't know which restaurant was better—upper or lower—so we decided earlier in the day to make reservations an hour apart in each one.

While eating at the restaurant on the lower level, which was nice, we finished eating and went upstairs to cancel the reservation. As we approached the maitre d', he said, "Two for lunch?" So we said, "Yeah." We showed him our badges, and he said, "Just show them to the waiter." The waiter approached us and went through the same rhetoric as the waiter downstairs, thus the double triple-lobster-tail lunch was born. So between us, we had a dozen lobster tails for lunch. We went to the casino, played a little roulette and the machines, and along came dinner. We said we wanted to try it again, so we made reservations in both upper and lower restaurants. Once again, it worked beautifully; and with the specials they had, we had another dozen lobster tails between us. This time, the waiter said, "What would you like to drink?" He handed us a wine list. I took one quick look and saw a nice thirty-dollar bottle of Sterling Sauvignon Blanc. We relaxed for a few hours and had another bottle of wine. So then the two little piggies went down to the casino and proceeded to win a couple of hundred. We went back to the hotel and stayed up all night, handicapping the next day's races.

On Thursday morning, we went early for breakfast and on to the tournament. We arrived at Cal Neva about two to three hours before the tournament to finish up our handicapping for the start of the tournament. While we were handicapping, we met a guy from Brooklyn, and he had already put in his ten bets for the day, unlike us, always watching where the most money goes just before the start of the race. We asked him why he put his bets in, and he said, "I'm leaving. My bets are in, and I'm done for the day."

I said, "Why do you do that?"

He said, "I'm from Brooklyn, New York."

"So are we."

He said, "Frankly, I don't want to be around when the races start."

I said, "Why is that?"

He said that the board at Aqueduct killed more horse players than all modern-day disasters. Touché.

On Thursday, Friday, and Saturday, during the tournament, we went up every lunch and dinner and ate two dozen lobster tails between us every day of the tournament. Four days at the tournament, double lunches, double dinners, a dozen lobster tails a day each, times that by four days, and do the math. Ninety-six lobster tails, drawn butter, fine wine, and we were totally fished out. It was a magnificent tournament, especially since we came home a few bucks ahead at the end. We were actually in first, second, and third place halfway through the tournament. We let it all hang out, trying to win the tournament, and finished up the track only a few bucks ahead. But it was all worthwhile; and subsequently, we went back a number of times.

For the return home, we followed a new route from Reno to the West Coast to the 5 freeway, Sacramento, and San Francisco. The reason we took an alternate route was too much ice and snow, and we did not want to go through the mountains again. We took the Donner Pass—another mistake. It was six of one, half a dozen of the other. Undulating like you wouldn't believe, Jimmy drove. It was around zero out, windchill was about 20 below and evening no less, dark out. It was icy out, really moving since we wanted to get home by five in the morning. I noticed up in the center of his console near the rearview mirror that he had a digital temperature gauge, and it was fluctuating between -5 and +5 and hovering around zero most of the time until we had a drop or rise in the road. Always trying to bet on something, and since there were no cockroaches, we started playing the game betting a buck a shot, watching the digital clock every minute as we went down. And on the top of the minute, he would call out "over or under," and I would have to make the call whether to take the bet or not, anticipating if he was on a rise or a dip in the road. The answer was on a dip, it would go below zero; on a rise, it would be positive. Anticipating this, I nailed him for about twelve bucks. I must say he put up a good battle, and he was up for a while but ultimately lost.

A Mortal Lock

I don't consider myself a very superstitious person. I don't necessarily believe in coincidences, but I do believe that having a great memory and the ability to recall past memories is a great asset when it comes to writing short stories. So I'll go back some sixteen years or so to 1999. Coincidentally, as you will read or have read, one of our lucky numbers was the number 9. My catchy little phrase "3-6-9 everything is mine" brings me to the subject—the year 1999 and the winner of that year's Kentucky Derby, Charismatic. 1999, three nines, Charismatic number sixteen in that year's Derby, giving you three nines and the six in sixteen in a roundabout way, we have the 3-6-9; superstitious, not really, it just happened to fall that way, ironically.

Actually, the numbers 3-6-9 went back to the early seventies when Jimmy, Lucy, Marion, and myself happened to win a number of exactas and trifectas in races at Saratoga with different combinations of 3-6-9. Well, come to think of it, maybe there's more superstition than I want to believe. Back in January and early February 1999, my friend Roger and I were sitting at the off-track racing facility in Indio, California, when Marion and I were living in Palm Springs. We started discussing possibilities of the upcoming Kentucky Derby in May. Roger and I both agreed that Answer Lively, the early favorite for the Derby, based on his winning the 1998 Breeders' Cup Juvenile, didn't seem to fit the bill. There were five or six horses at 3 or 4–1, and I thought the horse that ran third, a Wayne Lukas charge, might be a logical choice. Still, I was not thrilled with the possibilities, and I was always looking for something that could come on the scene and make some big money. After all, anybody can choose a favorite and go along with the crowd.

I always chose to make a statement. I always figure you don't go to the races, look to make a buck or two, and have lunch—just a walk in the park. Hitting a race for ten or twenty grand is what I consider putting a big smile on your face. May not be life changing, but sure as hell allows you some latitude.

I remember it like it was yesterday. Two or three weeks went by, and I sat down with Roger early that Saturday, February,19, 1999, still wondering who might come along and be a Derby horse. I told Roger I liked a long shot in the sixth race at Santa Anita. He kind of laughed at me. McAnally's horse, Apremont, was the best bet of the day, and the only horse that could beat him was the close second choice at 2–1, Forestry. At seven furlongs and only five horses in the field, he said, "The only long shot I see here, looking at his program, is Charismatic at 20–1, and he doesn't have a chance." I said, "I like Apremont, who is going to be the speed of the race. But if anything can run with him, it could set it up for a late run with Charismatic. I know seven furlongs is a little short, but if it happens, I think it could win or at least run second." He said, "This should be a piece of cake, Apremont/Forestry exacta box, no other way." He went on to bet it. I went to the windows, looking for a big score. I remember putting in a twenty-five-dollar Charismatic/Apremont exacta with a ten-dollar backup Apremont/ Charismatic exacta just in case Charismatic didn't win. No win bet. Roger said, "You're crazy." I said why. He said, "This is an allowance race at seven furlongs. Charismatic needs two turns, a mile and a half, and can't you read Charismatic's last race was a $62,500 claimer. And he ran second and moved up to win through a disqualification. So he only has one maiden win at $62,500 because his first two maiden special weights weren't competitive. When Lukas drops a young horse from maiden special weight to a maiden claimer, willing to lose the horse, I don't think the horse is any good."

I said, "Did you see that no one claimed him for $62,500?" He said yeah, he did. And I said, "Cagey Lukas didn't drop him to the basement at $30,000." He again said yeah. So I then explained that logic told me if he had dropped him to $30,000, someone may have taken a shot and claimed him, but it's another story at $62,500. Lukas got away with it and the horse won for fun.

The next few races, Lukas stepped him back up into allowances and minor stakes. Since Charismatic was a great-grandson of Secretariat, he thought he might try a one-mile turf event to see if turf was more to his liking. Turned out, it wasn't. His rider, Lafait Pincay, had ridden him exclusively. At his first few races at sprint distances, he failed trying to put the horse on the lead, and he did the same in the mile turf race. It was obvious, at least to me, that his breeding was not sprinting on the lead. Roger was right, he needed a mile and a half. His races early in his three-year-old campaign seemed to show he was able to close, and he was obviously filling out and becoming more of a racehorse. Still unable to win in allowance and minor stakes, he was beginning to close and become more competitive.

Lukas once again risked losing him. This time in $62,500, claiming the race for nonwinners of two races lifetime, and once again, there were no takers. The horse got in trouble trying to close in the race and ran second, and the eventual winner was disqualified and placed second; he was now a two-time winner. If he had not been interfered with, he would have pulled away and won by daylight. Being astute in the area of breeding, and having a propensity to delve back in the back breeding, since my younger days in the '50s and '60s, I pointed out to Roger certain quirks in Charismatic's breeding. Roger, being very knowledgeable also, began to take me somewhat seriously as I expounded before the race. One thing I firmly believe, and apparently all the gurus agree with, is that the mare brings a hell of a lot to the table when it comes to breeding. So I offered a ten-minute dissertation on Charismatic's breeding to Roger. "Take a good look at Charismatic. Who does he remind you of?" He said, "Don't play that game with me." He quickly agreed when I mentioned broad, reddish chestnut, white star dropping to a narrow blaze to somewhat of a snip at the bottom, and four white stockings. I said Secretariat and he sort of agreed. I went on to mention that he was a grandson of Weekend Surprise, who was a daughter of the great Secretariat, making him a great-grandson of Secretariat, who was the son of the great stallion Bold Ruler.

On the mare's side, Bali Babe's sire was What a Pleasure, who was a son of Bold Ruler. Other than the fact that Charismatic had four white stockings and Secretariat only three, lacking only the left front, they were like clones. Roger slowly started to understand, and as it approached post time for the sixth race, Charismatic had dropped to 17–1, and the race was off. Quickly, Apremont and Forestry went on to open an easy 5–6 length lead, and Apremont began to pull away as

Charismatic languished in last, some fifteen or twenty lengths behind. At the top of the stretch, as Apremont began to pull away, opening a 5–6 length lead in quick fractions, Charismatic picked it up and started to make his move. At the eighth pole, he was moving up with abandon, passing everyone in the field in a couple of strides and coming to the wire by two, putting away the rest of the field. Pincay kept riding him out past the finish line, working him an additional eighth of a mile and blowing by Apremont. I said to Roger, "Did you see that?" And he replied that Pincay worked him past the wire, and they were going to go to the Derby with this horse.

At the end of the day, after racing was over, I said, "Roger, that's my Derby horse."

He said, "Did you see the stakes race? My Derby horse is In Frank's Honor."

I said to him, "I'll bet you ten he doesn't win the Derby."

He asked, "How do you know that?"

I replied, "Look at your program. He's not nominated."

He said, "I guess you're right."

Now I had a dilemma. Understanding Wayne Lukas was also pointing to the Derby with another horse by the name of Cat Thief, who ran third as one of the favorites in last year's Breeders' Cup. What do I do? This horse was exactly what the doctor ordered, right in my wheelhouse—the second coming of Secretariat, long shot possibility for the Derby with a world-renowned trainer in Wayne Lukas and great rider Lafait Pincay. It looked like he was coming to hand, only trouble, was he an overachieving claiming horse or a diamond-in-the rough stakes-quality Derby hopeful?

Now being the end of February, and April beginning to come around, I kept my fingers crossed. Lukas will find a spot for this good-looking three-year-old. I began to wonder as the days rolled on with the Derby only some five weeks away. Another couple of weeks went by and still nothing. Finally, on the weekend of April 10 and 11, the racing form announced the field for the Coolmore Lexington stakes to be run at Keeneland the following Sunday, April 18, and Charismatic was entered. Having visited San Felipe, Mexico, previously, I asked Marion if she wanted to go; and then we could also put in a winter book bet on Charismatic to win the Derby. The winter book is a bet you can make on the Kentucky Derby in advance of the race starting around New Year's Day. In Mexico, there were certain advantages and disadvantages to making this wager. The semantics were that a printed list of approximately a couple of hundred Derby eligibles and their odds at the beginning of the year were listed, and you can put an advanced wager on any choice you wish. The list was usually headed by the winner of the Breeders' Cup Juvenile as one of the favorites, and based on their racing record, all the other horses nominated were listed in ascending odds. I knew who I wanted to bet and I was hoping to get big odds. The only place to bet the winter book was in Mexico, this and the fact that they only take a $1^1/_2$ percent takeout instead of the 15 percent or so in the United States was a great advantage. There was a downside, since only the top twenty earners could be entered for the Derby. All the rest—the other one to two hundred—fell by the wayside as the Derby approached. This happened simply because either they had not earned enough money to break into the top twenty; had gone down through injury, racing, or training; or simply, the owners or trainers decided to pass up on the Run for the Roses. If any of those situations occur, you simply lose your bet. To win your bet, you first have to make it into the field on the first Saturday in May—and if that is not enough, obviously, win it. That's why the odds were so great.

Knowing this, we set off on Friday, April 16, headed for the small town of San Felipe, today in the Baja on the Sea of Cortez. We were on a mission: relax in the sun on the seashore and spend a couple of days betting the ponies right next door at the off-track betting venue adjacent to our hotel, the El Conquistador. Knowing a few of the locals, two restauranteurs, Kiko and Domingo, we felt very comfortable. At one o'clock in the afternoon, racing began. Making a few wagers, I began to decipher the entries for the Derby in the winter book and noticed that Charismatic was entered at 50–1. I began to salivate. I thought that if I could win a few quid prior to the Lexington Stakes, I would parlay the winnings and bet Charismatic, who was listed in the Lexington Stakes at 20–1. The illusions of grandeur started to take over. I figured if I could be up a hundred going into the Lexington, parlay it on to Charismatic at 20–1, should Charismatic win paying forty dollars, I would have $2,000 to put on him in the winter book at 50–1. And should he win the Derby at 50–1, I'd win a cool hundred *g*'s. Simple—a piece of cake.

At three in the afternoon that sunny Sunday, my best-laid plans hadn't come to fruition. I started out the weekend with about $500 in my pocket less $200 for the hotel and meals—only $300 left at the start of racing and already down $100. I had $200 left. Adjusting my sights, being down a hundred instead of up a hundred, I only put twenty to win on him. He only went off at approximately 12–1 and won the race paying $26.20. More importantly, I wanted to see him do something against quality competition and do it in a way I thought the great Secretariat might have handled the field. I wanted him to break alertly instead of dead last, show some tactical speed, be placed in about the four or five path, splitting the field about mid pack, gradually moving up and taking the lead and pulling away in the stretch. A masterful ride by the great Jerry Bailey pulling away by two or three lengths at the wire. Bailey's agent must have seen exactly what I saw in this colt. Oh, I forgot to tell you one thing. The winter book odds change continuously. As horses win or lose races, so goes the odds for the Derby. This is advanced wagering.

Instantaneously, Charismatic took another step forward, and as he crossed the finish line, I sprang to my feet and quickly ran up to the window, hoping before the race was made official that I could capture the 50–1 odds on him in the Derby. I placed fifty to win on him, and to my astonishment, the odds already sank to 40–1. As the race became official, I decided to turn around and go back to the window and put another fifty to win. After all, 40–1 wasn't all that bad. I went back to my seat and began speaking to somebody, mentioning what I did and got 40–1 on him for the Derby. He replied, "That's great, but does he have enough earnings to be in the top twenty?" Then I thought for a second, *Uh oh!* This being April 18, three weeks from the Derby, there were no other races that he could run to earn more money. Now all I had to do was wait to see if he makes it into the Derby. Number 1, was he among the top twenty Thoroughbreds in earnings? Number 2, did his owner and trainer want to run in the Derby? Since he was trained by Lukas, who also had Cat Thief, it was somewhat questionable. And then all he had to do was win the race, a mere bag of shells.

The following weekend, sitting at the bar with Randy, Roger, and two young fellas that we didn't know all that well, we began to speak of the Derby and who everybody liked. I responded, "Charismatic is a mortal lock. Forget everything else." I was absolutely convinced that the way Charismatic was approaching the Derby was exactly textbook. Wayne Lukas, having been to so many Derbies had to know he had lightning in a bottle. The famous "they" say the Derby is won by the most well-prepared, the now horse, the Preakness, the fastest horse, and the third leg, the Belmont, and the best horse. Lukas had the best-prepared and now horse in his barn. When the entries came out on Derby week, there he was in the field—another battle won. Now all we had to do was draw a decent advantageous post position. When the entries came about, he was number 16. I was only hoping that he would draw a decent post position, not all that far on the outside. When there was one scratch, it left only nineteen to run, and Charismatic was coming out of the no. 11 post position. I could envision the running of the race prior to the race. I often do this in my mind's eye, anticipating how a horse will come out of the gate, where he or she will position themselves, how they'll rate, the time of the race, where they'll make their move, and how they will finish the race. I did exactly that the day of the Derby.

On Saturday morning, we went to breakfast about nine o'clock at OTB, which was almost a tradition. We met everybody there and started to handicap the race, since the racing form was available the previous day. And I had some ideas about how to attack the race itself. Since I already had a one-hundred-dollar win bet on Charismatic at 40–1 in Mexico, I was most interested in the exotics, exacta, trifecta, and superfecta. I spent all morning deciphering the horses I wanted to play. I wanted to play a superfecta, one over three horses, over three horses, over five horses. The easy one was Charismatic. The next three were tricky. Cat Thief, Lukas's other horse, Menifee and Vicar for second, and then repeat the same three for third and then add to Cat Thief, Menifee, Vicar, Timber Country, and Bob Baffert's colt-like filly, Excellent Meeting. Those were the horses that I eventually played. Strangely to my surprise, but not to my surprise, the *Daily Racing Form's* Chuck Klein had his selections for the entire card and stated his reasons for all his selections of the day. Shockingly, in the consensus column, there was Charismatic right on top in bold print as the best bet of the day. I said to myself, "There goes my price." I thought he was a mortal lock, and obviously, he did too. I expected to win!

After finishing breakfast, crowds started to come in. And with an empty chair at our table, an elderly woman, Mary Jane, introduced herself and asked for me, saying Randy the bartender directed her to our table. She said, "Who knows something about the races?" And he pointed us out. She asked if she could sit, and we said sure. I told her my thoughts. She said, "How sure are you? I only have about forty dollars." I said, "Tell you what to do, put ten on Charismatic and a two-dollar box on Charismatic and Cat Thief, and another two-dollar box on Charismatic and Menifee. That will cost you eighteen dollars." I had already put in my bets a half hour before. I boxed Charismatic with Cat Thief and Charismatic with Menifee and Charismatic with Vicar a few times each, and I put in trifectas with Charismatic on top over Cat Thief, Menifee, and Vicar a few times.

I sat there, finished up with Mary Jane and Marion, and I finally decided to go up and bet my superfectas, not realizing lines had started to get long. Taking too much time with Mary Jane, I rushed up and put in the numbers for the superfecta. As I was entering the fourth leg of Cat Thief, Menifee, Vicar, Prime Timber, and Excellent Meeting, the machine shut down and the race was off, never getting the bet in. My voucher in the amount of over $200 was about to play it multiple times.

As the gate opened, race caller Dave Johnson's first words were "Charismatic gets out nicely." I immediately thought we had a great shot. Then into the first turn, Charismatic had dropped back to about seventh but was still running well and with Cat Thief running on or near the lead. We were still confident, having great position. As the horses made their way around the track, Cat Thief was running exceptionally well. Charismatic had moved back up. And at the top of the stretch, he sat third and was about to make his winning move as Menifee was closing fast. At the wire, he held off Menifee with Cat Thief less than two lengths behind, finishing third followed by Timber Country and then Excellent Meeting fifth. Only Vicar was far back in the field.

Probably one of the best, if not the best handicapping we ever accomplished! Not only did we have the winner paying $63—with the exacta and trifecta paying over $700 and almost $6,000—but we also finished up fourth and fifth, making it virtually a clean sweep one through five. And just the thought makes me sick, thinking we came within seconds of hitting a one-dollar superfecta in excess of $26,000. Frankly, I can't tell you how many times we would have hit it. When I think back, it would have been at least five, maybe more, and projecting and running the numbers, five times $26K was over $130,000, if only for another minute. Although hitting for over $20,000 wasn't so bad.

No-Fly Zone

My wife and I were thinking about other funny, outrageous yarns that could be spun on a beautiful warm spring morning in anticipation of this year's Kentucky Derby and Triple Crown events. This story's a characterization of a great friend of ours, Roger Hergstrom, who passed away in 2014 in Southern California. He was privy to a number of the stories—some of which are contained in this manuscript and, unfortunately, a few others that were lost when our computer crashed in 2005. He's gone now, but his reaction to what he read at that time over ten years ago and what I'm about to have you readers experience would put a broad smile on his face.

When we first met Roger in the mid-'90s, we were all in our early fifties. He was thin, five-seven or so, wiry, maybe 120 or 130 pounds, and he was tending bar at an off-track wagering venue in Indio, California. Oddly, he said he had never had a drink in his life. I bought it hook, line, and sinker, saying to myself "sure." But as it turned out, it was true. He was born in Indiana, worked around Thoroughbreds, broke them, and was pretty damn knowledgeable when it came to selecting winners. While tending bar, just like most barkeeps, he accumulated many, many acquaintances along with a few select good friends over the years. From day to day, we would go down to play the races or watch them on the big screen at different intervals from around the country—races from Santa Anita, Hollywood Park, or Del Mar in Southern California. Bay Meadows, Golden Gate Fields in Northern California, Arlington Park in the Midwest, Aqueduct, Belmont, or Saratoga in the East. From race to race, track to track, the banter and camaraderie was continuous throughout the day and early evening. Roger would be serving drinks to all the locals and a number of notables that would come in regularly, such as George Blanda (retired Chicago Bears and Oakland Raiders quarterback) and Merv Griffin, his trainer Donny and entourage, the owners of Dutch Masters Farms, and local businesspeople. Some great stories were told back in those years. Tips would abound! I would take everything with a grain of salt. One afternoon, in the middle of the day, Roger walked over to our table where we were having lunch, and he said in a whisper, "Merv's got a good one." I said, "What race?" He said, "The no. 6 horse in the seventh race at Hollywood Park." Quite honestly, I don't remember the name of the horse. But I did look; and the horse was 3–1 the second choice. I turned to my program and put a line right through it. Roger asked what I was doing. I said I was throwing the horse out, and he said I was crazy, but I said no.

Roger insisted the horse had a great shot, and he should win. "This is a tip, by the owner."

I told Roger, "You never hear of a real tip." He asked what I meant by that. "First, it's an hour before the race. If you got the word, how many other people do you think got the word? When too many people get the word and bet the horse down from 3–1 to 4–5, the horse will get stiffed, no money in it. A real tip comes when the horse is 3–1 and eventually goes off at 5–1, and you get the tip with two minutes to post time. No matter how much money you play, you will really not change the odds, and the horse will return twelve dollars to win, the other way the horse pays $3.80. I know this because it's happened to me both ways too many times. I've smartened up over the years."

Sure enough, the no. 6 horse never got a call and ran next to last. I played the 2–1 favorite, who eventually went off at 3–1 and caught a nice winner.

Roger, as honest as they come, told me late one afternoon that he'd been offered a job by Merv, and I was happy for him since his job as a bartender was, at best, six to seven hours a day and, at minimum, scale plus tips—which still didn't amount to a hell of a lot. He began to tell me that he thought he caught a break with Merv. He would take Frank's position as Merv's general ranch hand; Frank was retiring. He quickly went over the facts that he would get $500 a week, a pickup truck, all gas and maintenance, and bed and board at the ranch. Understand this. Merv had his own chef, so when I speak about board, it was five-star gourmet every day. Incredible! It was better than hitting a monumental trifecta on the Derby.

You may ask the question, how did he get on Merv's shortlist? As I said, Frank was retiring. One day, Frank, a robust Mexican always wearing his ten-gallon cowboy hat put in a bet at one of the machines in the rear screened-in patio area where Roger would constantly be ducking in and out to have a cigarette. As luck would have it, as Roger put in his bet, he looked down and there were a couple of tickets sitting there—most likely losers that Frank left there from the previous race. He quickly scanned them. One ticket was a one-dollar combination ticket and looked like a winner; and as he looked further, he recognized it was indeed a winner. He ran over to Frank and asked him what horses he played in the last race. Roger said, "Frank, you threw away a winner here." Roger walked him over to the machine, put the ticket in, and it came up over $4,800. Frank never forgot that, and when asked by Merv if he would recommend anybody for the job, he quickly mentioned Roger's name. And so it was.

Sometimes it's better to be lucky than good; and when you're both, that's an added advantage. Roger did a lot of general work during the day at the ranch, and there was only one major contingency with the job. No matter what—when and if Merv called—he would have to drop everything and ascribe to the order of the day. Ninety-nine percent of the time, it would be a call to pick up Merv at whatever the airport was where he was landing.

During the time he worked for Merv, he would occasionally mention in passing that he had a definite fear of flying, and since he was in and out of airports, the subject would come up. Through the years, Merv was always after the elusive Kentucky Derby horse. I remember two very well. The first one was a grey colt by a stallion named Freehouse. The horse was a nice horse in his two-year-old campaign, and Merv started pointing him in the rigorous direction of the Kentucky Derby. Roger was thrilled, always saying, "We're going to the Derby. Merv's got a horse this year." But, the Freehouse colt went bad in the early spring of that year, and Roger's hopes of going to the Derby in Louisville, Kentucky were dashed. Subsequently, in 2005, Merv had a two-year-old named Stevie Wonder Boy, who ran in the Breeders' Cup Juvenile, went off at 9–2, and won the race, notoriously becoming the early-morning line Kentucky Derby favorite for 2006. Once again, hopes were alive and well in Southern California.

In 2005, we returned to Long Island, leaving Palm Springs in July of that year. I remember speaking to Roger at the time of the Breeders' Cup of '05 and discussing Merv's horse, and Roger said, "Merv's agent, Dennis Ward, said he's going to be a good one and said they had a big shot at the Breeders' Cup and, hopefully, a Derby horse." Now that was good information, and I made a hunk of change keying him in the pick three. Third race, Folklore at even money; fourth race, Stevie Wonder Boy at 9–2; and fifth race, Intercontinental at 15–1, with Ouija Board second at odds-on, but failing to hit the pick four with best bet of the year, Lost in the Fog, at 3–5. The pick four projection 1–1, 9–2, 15–1, and 1–9 was the favorite pick four, paying over $1,600 for every one dollar. We had that twenty times, looking for a grand slam. We could have had a grand slam by wheeling all the horses in that race for one or two dollars. The bet we made would have returned over 32 *g*'s. Lost in the Fog, a front runner, got off bad, made the lead at the top of the stretch, and was swallowed up, finishing seventh at the wire, beaten by Silver Train, paying $25.20 and completing the one-dollar pick four for $13,162.00.

After that Breeders' Cup, Merv started to make plans for the Derby. Roger was happy—exuberant, to say the least. A couple of months went by, and I gave Roger a call to see how he was doing. It was around the holiday season, and I remember saying "How's Stevie Wonder Boy doing?" I figured he'd be all hopped up and getting ready for an excursion to the Kentucky Derby since he previously mentioned that Merv was making plans to take everybody to the Derby with him. He said, "I'm not with Merv anymore." I said, "What are you talking about? You were all happy about getting to the Derby." He said, "I told Merv I quit just a week ago." I asked why. Roger told me Merv came to him and said, "Listen, I'm trying to make plans. Should we get lucky and get to the Derby, I'm going to need someone to stay here at the ranch and take care of things, so I've decided that you would be the nominee."

Then Roger said, "How do you like that? I told him I quit."

I said, "Roger, you told me a million times you would never fly. You have never been on a plane. I even asked you to fly out to Kennedy Airport and we would go to Saratoga since you always wanted to see Saratoga, and you said 'no way no how.' And I remember you telling me that you mentioned this a number of times to Merv whenever you picked him up at the airport. He must have remembered, and therefore, you were the logical choice to stay behind. That's a no-brainer."

Suddenly, there were a few seconds of silence. I said, "Roger, are you there?"

"Yeah," he said, "but he could have asked anyway."

Ussery's Alley

The day before Super Bowl 2009, Saturday, January 31 started out pretty much as others have. By the way, please patronize me as I have been known to go on and on and on and on, on occasion. Bobby, if I may, I believe in my heart of hearts that this little "Ha! Ha!" story might just capture you. Hopefully, not only you, but also my son's friend, Kenny; his wife, Allie; and their young son, Jackson, eventually; and your friend, Allie's father.

I know this is an awful lot of superfluous info, but what the hell, you only live once, so I hope you'll appreciate the effort.

Please let me set the stage. Saturday afternoon, the day before the Super Bowl, was my grandson Jake's third birthday party. We all had a great time at the ice cream parlor. At late afternoon, Kenny, Allie, and Jackson were saying good-bye. Kenny was aware through my son, James, that I had been involved with Thoroughbreds. Just before he was exiting, he asked my wife and I a question. "My father-in-law lives down in Florida, and he has a very good friend. Maybe you know him. He's an ex-jockey." Kenny stopped. I looked at him and I said, "OK, spit it out. Who is he?" Kenny said, "Robert, uh Bobby," and slowly said your last name, Ussery, and reiterated, "Bobby Ussery."

It blew my mind. Of all people, I thought he was going to say a no-name, and as you know, there were many of them. But instead, I almost fell down. I had this grin on my face like the cat that ate the canary, and Kenny and his wife were shocked/amazed that I was aware of you. As a matter of fact, with a smile on his face, Kenny said we had to come down to Florida and hang out with you. My mind trended back fifty years in a heartbeat like it was yesterday—complete, absolute, and total recall.

As I said, I can be long winded, but not with hot air. If you will, I will just whet your appetite today in hopes of some additional back barn banter in the future.

Most historians, racetrackers, and aficionados in any position might try to impress you with common knowledge. Poo, poo, not me! Neither I nor you have the time for that. Many years later, I thank you for the opportunity to congratulate you on all your great victories, and even more so, seeing all those great front-running rides for which you were so famous. May I take the time to reminisce about one up you had over forty years ago in the late spring of the early sixties.

It was the one and only time in my life that I heard Freddie "Cappy" Capossela blow the call. I really hope you heard it. I know on occasion over the loudspeaker that you, as a jockey, may have heard the call. I would almost lay the odds, in retrospect, that it was a Saturday, late spring, early sixties, sixth race $20K/$30K claimer or NW1/NW2 allowance. That day, you rode no. 3, Audience, and Eric Guerin rode no. 2, Batu. Hopefully, I am not having a senior moment with the numbers and conditions. Absolutely, no question, one of the greatest duels of all time. Never mind all that rhetoric about Alydar and Affirmed. Cappy called only seven horses in the field. He was kind of stuttering, stammering, and silent for what seemed to be forever. It was only two, maybe three seconds at most, and being the 9–5 choice, he couldn't find you. He called Batu and Batu only by 1½. Batu opened the lead by 2½, 3 on the backstretch. He called all the others and realized he couldn't find you aboard Audience. On top of the grandstand, he again called Batu, going into the turn. That's the only call he made at 5/8 pole, the 1/2, the 3/8, and 1/4. Not until the 3/16, approaching the top of the stretch, did Cappy see a double image and realize where you were. At that point, not only nose to nose, head to head, neck to neck, withers to withers, striding in complete synchronization, you came down the stretch, and on that glorious day, you both hit the wire simultaneously. And I, along with many others, including Cappy, had to wait for what seemed like forever—at least eight to nine minutes, without a doubt, to put your number up. I was there. I had ten dollars to win on Batu. I hate to admit it, but I'll never forget it. You went on to be depicted on a future Aqueduct full-color racing program cover with, again, those senior moments: 12–16 wins, if I remember correctly, on claimer of the year Audience.

Bobby, or Mr. Ussery, should I say, I am very familiar with many of your exploits—Proud Clarion, Dancer's Image, Peter Fuller, John Galbraith, Dan Galbraith, Darby Dan Farm, John Phillips, Kentucky, Lexington, Louisville, Saratoga, all the venues, all the tracks, farms, sales pavilions, Fasig-Tipton, Barrett's, and others. All this did not amount to a hill of beans, unless you recall, share, and enjoy that gift with good friends and others, new or old. I hope this little jaunt down memory lane has pleased you, for it most certainly has been my pleasure.

I decided to incorporate this story, meant to be written for and delivered to Bobby Ussery himself, worthy of mention. So I say what the hell. By the way, I did get a chance to speak with Bobby to ask him a question or two. I contacted him, not realizing I had been given his cell phone and caught him at Home Depot in some unknown part of Florida, doing daily chores. He actually had the courtesy to speak with me for ten or fifteen minutes. I asked him if he recalled the race. Thinking back, I believe he did. So I asked him the question. I said I believed that at certain times, when there was a strong wind down the backstretch, that the riders may have actually been able to vaguely hear the race call during the race. So I asked if he actually heard Freddy blow the call of the race, not mentioning the speed duel between his horse, Audience, and Batu. His answer was simply, flatly, no. Come to think of it, it was kind of a stupid question, and I should have known better, being an ex-athlete. In the heat of competition and his concentration on the race, thundering hooves on the attack, how could he!

Playing the Odds

I have found that every racetrack was different, both esthetically and technologically—from the days of the old Jamaica, Belmont, and Saratoga tracks in New York, to Hialeah and Gulfstream in Florida, to Tropical Park, Santa Anita, Hollywood Park, Del Mar in Southern California, and to Agua Caliente in Tijuana, Mexico—beautiful and as colorful as they were, and in some cases were in their day, they were all quite different with their track compositions, configurations, sizes, and many other peculiarities. All these differences added to small differences, making all the difference between winning or losing at the track.

Owners, trainers, jockeys, and especially the horses sense these differences. A good handicapper will use these as his or her tools of the trade. These are the known standards of handicapping winners. I recognize a few other tools of the trade. After speaking with a few friends over the years, I found one very useful tool. Since approximately 1980, many of my friends who played the ponies said they no longer had the inclination to buck the crowds on big racing days like Kentucky Derby, Preakness, Belmont, Breeders' Cup days, and such. Big mistake! Such events, whether it was the Saratoga meet in New York in August or Del Mar in California, offer incredible overlays. The old adage "horses for courses" comes into play. I absolutely believe they sense their surroundings; they're either happy or they're not, and will either excel, move up, or win when entered at certain tracks that they relish. I've seen the phenomenon happen year after year at all the tracks I've been to, and if you don't think trainers and owners use this strategy to a fare thee well, we are not living on the same planet. Consider the connection of the horse, meaning owner, trainer, rider, along with a switch to a favorable track. Most importantly, the new era of exceptionally large fields can number beyond the normal twelve-stall starting gate, along with an auxiliary eight-stall starting gate, at times creating a cavalry charge, and most importantly, bringing crowds to the racetrack. These crowds create such overlays that it is beyond belief, and they are just there for the pleasure of seeing the horses run, playing lucky numbers, children's birthdays, anniversaries, or telephone numbers. There is no rhyme or reason creating the big overlays. These wonderful novices gladly hand their money over to me. As quoted in old scripture, "Forgive them, Lord, for they know not what they do," and thank you all.

With para-mutual wagering, exacerbating the allure of super exotic wagering, the simple fact is many horses will go off at incredibly lucrative odds. I can't tell you how many times I've looked at horses that could not virtually lose and should have paid odds of even money or 2–1, light up the board, winning at 4 or 5–1, or better. So many times, my wife and myself and a few close friends will endure the crowds, enjoy the day, and walk away very satisfied. Some outstanding winners that I recall over the years were winning the Belmont Stakes with Quadrangle in 1964, when the Belmont was run at Aqueduct while Belmont was being renovated, catching the Little Roman Brother defeating the great Kelso at Saratoga, "the first million-dollar earner in racing history" when all the major stakes races were purses topping out at only $100,000. Seeing, playing, and watching Hall of Fame trainer, the great H. Allen Jerkens, "the giant killer," defeat Secretariat twice with Onion and Prove Out at Saratoga and Belmont at big odds. Also, seeing Beau Purple, owned by Jack Dreyfuss, defeat a few great ones a number of times.

Another great day was in early June, in the 1971 Belmont. I loved the horse named Pass Catcher. Everyone thought I was crazy. Trainer Eddie Yowel had just lost to Bold Reasoning a week earlier in the Jersey Derby. I loved Bold Reasoning in that race. Walter "Mousey" Blum was in Pass Catcher's irons. Bold Reasoning, in my estimation, was the fastest horse in America at that time. Pass Catcher had the lead in that race by two lengths, finally caving in the last eighth. Why in God's name was Eddie Yowel racing back one week later in the Belmont Stakes at a mile and a half? Simple. He had lightning in a bottle, and he went on to win the race by two, taking virtually the same route that Greentree Stable took in 1968 with Stage Door Johnny, a virtual unknown who came to hand nine days earlier in winning the Peter Pan Stakes at a mile over the same Belmont racing strip. I couldn't believe Pass Catcher was going off at 35–1, and the exacta was very, very simple, just box him and Johnny Campo's odds-on favorite entry of Am'behaving and Jim French, a nice win bet and exacta bet and a big score when Pass Catcher came romping home, paying seventy-two dollars to win.

Come to think of it, these scenarios played out more often than you want to believe. You just have to take the game seriously and have a good memory, and all this doesn't matter unless you have the conviction to put your money where your mouth is. Yes, you're right, Bold Reasoning eventually sired a dark bay paddle foot colt in 1974 for $16,500, who was purchased at a yearling sale by Jim Hill, Karen, and Mickey Taylor, and trained by Billy Turner, by the name of Seattle Slew, the first and only undefeated Triple Crown winner. He was only equaled in 2015 by American Pharoah.

My wife and myself formed Pacific Coast Stables in California in 1988, just a decade or so after. And just letting my mind wander, it would have been nice to be at the above-mentioned sale in 1975, and knowing how good Bold Reasoning, sired by Boldnesian, son of the famous Bold Ruler, how could Seattle Slew have gone that inexpensively? This is just a small sampling of the many great horses, experiences, and fun times we've had through the years. Oh, did I forget to say extremely profitable?

The Sport of Kings

Away from the computer for virtually a month, it is now Memorial Day weekend 2015. On a bit more serious note, this day, Sunday, May 24, after wrestling and, without a doubt, losing sleep and overthinking this entire project, I have finally decided to take a stand and put it to rest. An enormous amount of time and effort had brought me to make these assessments of the Thoroughbred industry and everything surrounding the sport of kings. Many have probably forgotten why they call it the sport of kings, and that's exactly verbatim, word-for-word, the truth behind the story. For decades, dating back over a century and a half, only those rich enough could actually afford to dabble in this sport. It was such a closed society. At one time, they set the rules and engaged in the game, not permitting outsiders to enter their world. Yes, there were stakes races for the most well-bred animals of the day, allowance races, and at the bottom of the heap were the claiming races. If you were fortunate enough to afford a quality Thoroughbred and acquire the services of a trainer willing to take on the responsibility of training, talk to jockeys' agents to acquire his services to ride, and meet the qualifications of the conditions book, and pull into the race itself, then you became the proud owner of a starter. Whatever level you were committed to—whether it be stakes, allowance, or claiming competition—you finally had a fighting chance. Now let's take a closer look at the lower entry level of the claiming divisions. Depending on whether or not you're racing at a major venue or a smaller country track, the numbers were dramatically different a century ago.

For every major event on the race card, there were usually eight other lesser events, and most of those were and still are claiming races.

In the fifties era, grade 1 stakes races had a purse of $100,000 for top-level competition (today $1,000,000, to $3,000,000,), and the lower-level claiming races in the fifties $2,000 to $5,000 (today $50,000 to $100,000). *Inflation*!

As the Industrial Revolution progressed—horses to automobiles, trains to planes, and finally landing on the moon—and after the Korean War and the Vietnam conflict, affluence began proliferating. Old money will forever be ingrained in society. Today's new money and entrepreneurial spirit rising to the fore brought a new player to the game. Those few who could afford the luxury of well-bred equine creatures would find themselves at a Fasig-Tipton or Barretts sales auction at the likes of Saratoga, Keeneland, and Del Mar. Others would venture into the claiming game. They could no longer hold these individuals back, so open claiming was born. Though you could claim a horse, it wasn't all that easy and certainly not inexpensive. You see, it was a catch-22. Every racetrack had what they called a meet. That meet could be defined as a 57-day spring meet, a 106-day summer meet, or an 82-day fall meet. This described the number of racing days and time of year. To qualify, you must put a claim in the claim box at the clerk's office no later than fifteen minutes prior to the race and have sufficient funds in your horsemen's account to cover the claiming price. Aha, one other small issue back in the day was that you could not put a claim in for a horse if you had not raced a horse at the given meet. So, being a newbie, I guess you couldn't make a claim. But aha, once again, simply engage a trainer and speak to him about claiming one for you since, obviously, he has raced a horse at the meet and he is able to claim one for you under his name. Since the racing form comes out seventy-two hours early, horses have to be entered prior to the printing of the racing form, so you actually should have approximately seventy-two hours to make that decision.

So let's set the stage. You're getting an education. Let's say you have an eye on a certain horse, and arbitrarily, he's going to run in the fourth race on Saturday. The claiming price is for $50,000. Your trainer puts the claim in—obviously, with the promise that he will get to train your horse at his daily rate of $100 per day, which is "inexpensive for today." But the State steps in after the claim and asks for their $4,000–$5,000 use tax for the purchase of a retail commodity. Then the trainer decides to transfer the horse back to your name so he can race in your name and colors, for your trainer does not want to be stuck paying taxes on any prospective winnings. And of course, your own vanity issues sound like a good idea. Another transfer, another $4,000–$5,000 sales tax. So being successful has now cost you close to $60,000. It is not for the faint of heart.

I mentioned the above date. This year's Belmont will be run on Saturday, June 6. I honestly hope there will be a Triple Crown winner. Frankly, the country has been starved too long. I remember when *Secretariat* came along in 1973, and it was twenty-five years from the previous Triple Crown winner in 1948, *Citation*. it is now thirty-seven years since Affirmed won the last Triple Crown; it is time. *American Pharaoh* looks like the real deal, but taking all the facts into consideration, and even after he has completed a great run to win the Kentucky Derby from an almost impossible post position (18) and then winning the Preakness, which appeared to be with incredible ease, I still have my doubts. Here are my reasons. Let's go back to 2012, approximately twenty thousand Thoroughbreds were foaled. This year, 2015, over twenty-two thousand were foaled and registered with the Jockey Club in North America. Just taking the sheer numbers, even allowing half fillies (although usually 99 percent of the time not considered for the Triple Crown), it seems to me an almost impossibility to conceive any one of these beautiful creatures could win a Kentucky Derby (the odds are so great against that possibility) and then go on to win the second jewel, the Preakness—much less the entire trifecta, the Belmont. And now it has come to the almost impossible task of happening again for the twelfth time. Triple Crown winner. Every star has to line up so perfectly from the day he is foaled to the day the gate opens at Belmont. Just the slightest miscue at any stage of the past three-plus years, and the whole thing goes up in a puff of smoke. Every time this powerful 1,200-pound animal puts a hoof on the track for a morning workout, the trainer, the exercise rider, the hot walker, and the owner have to cross their fingers and hope nothing goes wrong. And those, my friends, are the daily problems that arise every morning. And just to look a little deeper, I've seen the best, and I honestly question the breeding. I just hope at the end of the day, when the bell rings and the gates open and they're off and running, that his head is not turned, that he's standing erect, and he's looking forward, and that he doesn't get bumped coming out of the gate or during the course of the race, because it could all be over in a heartbeat—the veritable New York moment!

The Garden State Mudder

I was on a mission. Sometimes, I do my best work when I can't sleep. So 5:05 a.m., February 4, 2016, finds me writing this story. It is two days after Jake, my eldest grandson's tenth birthday. We were still at the Ski Village. My grandson, his sister, my son, and daughter-in-law have all left for home. I have completed "Eunice, the Elusive Pink Unicorn," and I am starting this new story.

I was thinking of my friend Jimmy in California. My wife and myself have just recently put together an itinerary for a four-week, West Coast vacation, starting on June 28, 2016. We are traveling from San Francisco to Palm Springs, approximately six hundred miles along the coast highway, visiting friends along the way, including Jimmy, among others. Just last week, we found out he may be moving to Florida. This is new, since two weeks ago, he said, "I'll see you then." What gives?

Awake, not being able to sleep, I thought I would sneak downstairs and write since I had a good story and was chomping at the bit to get started, even at this ungodly hour.

Back in '63, Jim and I were repoing for a living, working out of Lynbrook, Long Island, New York. Interesting job, might become dangerous at times, but since we were Superman, Batman, and Robin wrapped in one, it was always a piece of cake. All I can remember about this hilarious day was that not having much business on Long Island, or for that matter, New York, we decided to run over to New Jersey. Thirty minutes, twenty-five cents, over the Fifty-Ninth Street Bridge and Holland Tunnel, we would be in what we considered the bowels of the earth. We had a couple of items to repo for Sears and thought we could pick up forty to fifty dollars (good money, considering the times) then shoot on back to Aqueduct and parlay it into a couple of hundred, always thinking big.

It was early on a Saturday morning. We repoed the items, shot back to pick up the gelt, and still made the daily double at the Big A: a brilliant plan. The only thing was at about 9:30 a.m., we passed a sign that said "Horseback Riding $5.00 an hour," with an arrow pointed to the stables. I said, "Let's ride for an hour." Jimmy agreed, but only one hour. It was cool, about forty-five degrees. It had rained hard Friday, but it was sunny that day. The stable had saddled up two, pointed out where to ride, and we were off.

It was muddy; a number of large puddles were between us and an outdoor drive-in theater. My horse wanted to run, and I accommodated. He took off into a full gallop. Jimmy's didn't want any part of it. For a minute or so, I looked around. Jimmy was nowhere to be found. I was having a ball, weaving in and out of the drive-in speakers, up and down the undulating gravel rows where the cars parked. When I looked back in the general direction of where Jim would be, I saw him way over there. I could hear him yelling at the horse to move. I returned to join him, and I couldn't believe what I saw. There was Jim, sitting in the saddle, his horse sitting in a two-foot-deep puddle, sloshing around in the dirty muddy water. A sight to behold. I was laughing my ass off, but Jim wasn't so thrilled. Fifty-three years later, I'm still laughing. I wish I had a camera that day. Always with a grin, he always denies the story.

It's now between the Derby and the Preakness, mid-May, attempting and successfully editing this story from February. I'll add a bit more. Now I realize that I may have had the last laugh that day, but I realize subsequently that he may really have had the last laugh.

About a year or two later, after his ride on the mudder, we went to the riding stable in Long Beach on New Year's Day. After drinking all night, we were half in the bag. We finally got there, and there were two horses available for riding. The stable hand quickly tacked one up, handed me the reins, and said to Jim that he would have to wait for one to come back in.

Jim said, "What about the big gray?"

The stable hand said, "Nobody rides him." Standing sixteen hands plus and kind of a rogue, they were apprehensive about putting somebody on his back. I was off about ten or fifteen feet, waiting for one to come back. My friend said, "My buddy can ride anything. Saddle him up."

So he did. He called me back and said, "Your buddy says you can ride anything."

So I walked him out from underneath the boardwalk where they were stabled, got a leg up, and started to walk down to the water's edge. My gray was a little stubborn, wanting to turn around, but I kept him moving forward down near the water. After a few minutes, he half-assed reared up, and my steed bolted for the stalls, tucked his head, and it became impossible to pull him up. The more I pulled, the tougher he got. And the only thing that saved me from taking a header under the boardwalk was the fact that I jerked him quickly to the left and bailed off as he went right back to his stall under the boardwalk. Standing on the beach sand, I saw my friend Jimmy smiling and cantering back. He said, "Gotcha! Never laugh at me again. That's payback for the mudder."

Now in the middle of May 2016, Jim and his new bride, Siri, have trekked their way to Florida on the East Coast; and now he is talking about Saratoga this year. So, so be it for a visit to him in California this summer. One for one each on the gotchas I believe he has long forgotten. I haven't, so I will have one in store, most likely in our old venue when we meet in Saratoga in August.

Horse People

In anticipation of a blizzard coming, I had a few moments to reflect and put this story on paper. Thinking of Jonathan Smart, I spoke to him a number of times this past year. After all, who better to speak with since this connects the dots between stories—this as I'm writing "The Handicapper's Challenge," Yaw, and other unique situations. Jonathan Smart, in my humble opinion, is one of the most genuine and talented steeplechase riders I have experienced in over half a century in the sport of racing. Now let's take it back a notch. As much as I know about him and have spoken with him, we have never actually personally crossed paths. I owe him a drink, and one day, we shall certainly meet, since our only tête-à-tête had been by phone. My wife had a good laugh as she overheard my conversation with Jonathan. For lack of a better phrase, I mentioned to Jonathan, in his fifties and I his senior, number one item on my bucket list ironically, since I have firsthand experience on handling Thoroughbreds, I would want to accomplish my burning desire to jump a few hedges. As we spoke, we started getting into the minutiae in terms of horsemanship. I told him I was still extremely agile and had great strength in my hands and super balance. Surprisingly, he took the bull by the horns (or should I say "the reins"), and in response, he said to me, "You know going over the jumps, you have to grab the horse's mane to remain in the saddle." I said, "Of course, reins in hand, you don't want to set the bit back and put him or her on the bit. You have to virtually become part of the well-oiled machine under the saddle." I told Jonathan that I had a great rapport with the animals. They responded extremely well to my touch and my voice. As a matter of fact, in over fifty years, I've never been stepped upon, bitten, or nipped, or even come close to any adverse situation with any one of them stallions, colts, fillies, or mares. Albeit, I remember one stallion did pin his ears back once; that has been the total extent of it. Strangely, in response, Jonathan said, "I wish I could say that."

Remember, it's always a people-to-people world. So if you can articulate and carry yourself and not be intimidated by anyone, it is amazing—the friendships you can develop along the way. At the expense of mentioning that previous tale in "The Handicapper's Challenge," I will mention this. I first became aware of Jonathan back in the late eighties or early nineties. English-born Jonathan, at the tender age of twenty-five, led the jockey standings with twenty-five wins. Truthfully, I'm not quite sure what year that would have been, but it was probably in the seventies. Not getting too personal, but I'll take a wild guess and say those twenty-five wins he had at that time, I couldn't tell you whether that was here in the States or overseas. Since my first recollection concerning Jonathan was when he was riding for the likes of Hall of Fame turf and steeplechase trainer Jonathan Sheppard here in the good old United States of America—and, coincidentally, not knowing all the horses he rode—I couldn't tell you if they were world-beaters or old $5,000 claimers. Nonetheless, I proudly consider him my friend.

Oddly, thinking back on my first experience with steeplechase racing, it could have been the first, second, or third time I wagered a few quid on such a race. It was at Aqueduct Racetrack in New York. There were some ten horses entered. In those days, there was only win, place, show, and daily double wagering. I remember betting four dollars to win on a gallant steed at 7–1. At the second hedge, on the first turn, three horses went down along the backstretch; and just before entering the far turn, another two horses went down. In the stretch, the first time I was looking, my horse, no. 3, was still part of the remaining five, going past the finish line the first time. Two more horses go down, and I was yelling to my friend Jimmy, "I'm still up." He looked at me in amazement. We still had a big shot at the race. Albeit, racing third but still in the hunt, they went down the backstretch for the final time. A 15–1 shot was leading by three or four lengths, and we were battling it out for the runner-up position. And Jimmy said to me, "Thanks for coming up with that horse," since he put a few bucks on it himself. Halfway through the final turn, our horse left the other one in the dust and began to pull astride the 15–1 shot and started to pull away and went on to spread eagle the other two with one jump remaining, and we crossed our fingers that we wouldn't go down and would finish the race—which we did by some ten lengths. That is one story I have yet to mention to Jonathan.

Jonathan was more than likely aboard a number of great horses for Jonathan Sheppard, primary trainer over the decades for Augustin Stables. I don't know that particular list, but I'm sure there were many in his younger days, and I'm sure at many different venues of racing. This last phone conversation I had with him in January, I was looking forward to speaking with not only him but also with Jonathan Sheppard and his secretary, Lisa, at Kennett Square, Pennsylvania, just to acknowledge this story including him. As a matter of fact, I had asked Jonathan Smart if he was going to be at the Radnor Hunt Club this spring, the third Saturday in May, for the races. He said, "Probably not since it's a long haul from Aiken, South Carolina, but you might run into Jonathan Sheppard there." I think this week, I shall give him and/or Lisa a holler at Kennett Square and thank her for mentioning my name to Jonathan Sheppard, who, coincidentally, asked Jonathan Smart to field my original call in response to my call, trying to do my detective work about his horse Yaw and the race he ran in the late eighties, which was the whole center of these few stories that I am now writing. Kudos to both Jonathan and Lisa.

One last question. Did Jonathan Sheppard connect the dots between himself, Yaw, Jonathan Smart, and me—incorporating everything in the big ball of wax I am working on? Thank you all.

Jonathan Smart, Marion and Catherine French Executive Director of Steeplechase Museum Camden, SC home of the prestigious Colonial Cup.

Chuck galloping Thoroughbred on training track at
Pacific Coast Stables, Winchester, Ca 1992

Eunice, the Elusive Pink Unicorn

On the twenty-ninth of January 2016, Marion and I had been invited and were eagerly waiting to travel to Treetop Villas at Shawnee in the Poconos. We were invited for a winter sports weekend with our son, James; daughter-in-law, Diana; nine-year-old Jake; and itsy-bitsy, teeny-weeny Rylie, only four. Teeny-weeny, yes—but an outrageous handful nonetheless. You must be wondering, as we speak, why this story and what a pink unicorn has to do with it. Well, to me, it was one of those six-second no-brainers to name the story. Ever since we hit the highways, I knew I had an absolute agenda in mind. It all came to fruition on Friday evening, when we met the younger ones, their friends, two other couples along with their children, and one exchange student—totaling a horde of nine in all, enough to field a baseball team. My agenda was to find a way, time permitting, to bring Jake and Rylie to the riding stables and at least have them get acquainted with the equine experience.

The window appeared. Jake and James were occupied all Saturday and Sunday on the ski slopes. The rest of us—Diana, Rylie, my wife's sister Annette, me, and my wife—all went tubing. Everyone had a blast, especially the little one. We took pictures and videos of all of us and also the snowboarding. About one or two in the early afternoon, we were all returning to our lodge-like villa, and we asked if it was okay to take the kids to the stables for a quick look-see. The parents said yes, and we were off to find the elusive pink unicorn. This weekend was especially significant since on the following Tuesday, February 2, Jake (Punxsutawney) would turn ten; so the weekend was somewhat of a birthday surprise.

At the stables, we engaged a young man by the name of Casey, who asked if he could help us. We got into a conversation, and I told him that I probably would be the only one riding, and that would be during the week since everyone else had to go back to work in New York. Marion and I were staying, and I would probably leg up during the week. He mentioned they were a family-owned business, and I spoke to him about my experiences around the animals. I asked my wife to take the kids and show them around, take some pictures, and we would take them riding when it was more convenient. Rylie asked Casey, "Where is my unicorn, and what is his name?" Casey said, "Who?"

Rylie said, "The pink unicorn, silly."

Casey said, "Her name is Eunice."

I said, "She's probably hiding. They're very hard to find."

After looking high and low, spending at least fifteen to twenty minutes calling for the unicorn, it was about time for us to leave. Rylie really wanted to see her unicorn, so I said, "Let's go and see Casey. Maybe he knows."

He said, "Gee, I haven't seen her all day. She must be out there romping with the other unicorns out in the forest, but it's extremely hard because if you ever see one, they vanish in a heartbeat."

I said, "I think we have to leave, and maybe we'll see you again someday."

Breakfast at Belmont and Saratoga

It was a beautiful weekday afternoon, temperature in the mid-70s, late May 2016, a couple of weeks before the Belmont Stakes. Nyquist had just won the Kentucky Derby and followed up with a third-place finish in the Preakness this past Saturday. My wife and I were at my oldest son James's house for his forty-second birthday. Having a party with friends and relatives, I came up with a bright idea about racing since the subject somehow always came up, and especially at the time of the Triple Crown races. After all, my son was born the weekend of the Preakness, when JR's Pet beat Little Current in that year's renewal. Since my wife and I had taken our two boys, James and Brian, to breakfast at Belmont when they were about five or six, I thought it would be a great idea, and the time was definitely right to take our four grandchildren—Jake (ten years old), Chase (eight years old), Graham (seven years old), and Rylie (four years old)—and repeat the event and establish a generational event. It's hard to get everybody together and make an attempt in this day and age to pull this off successfully. Not knowing if the kiddies would be thrilled, the immediate acceptance of this was through the roof, I'm happy to say. My wife and I haven't been to breakfast at either venue since 2007, when we were at Saratoga during the Fasig-Tipton yearling sales. We were not only going to enjoy everything, but we would also see the children's expressions when they saw the horses working out on the track. I would be taking pictures in an attempt to capture the majesty of it all that might be used in creating the cover of this book.

I thought it might be very interesting and informative to bring forth a new generation to enjoy the love of the Thoroughbred and knocking off a plethora of birds with one stone.

With this final story, I project that Thoroughbred racing will thrive when people get to understand the purity of the game itself. Where else can you go for a few dollars, enjoy an afternoon of fresh air under the canopy of trees in a country-like setting, watch a few races, and see one of these impressive equines in full flight? They would be striding out and running a hole in the wind, reaching out to hit the wire first under an exuberant jockey, celebrating waving his stick in the air in triumph. So take the family and spend and enjoy a day in an environment where the Thoroughbred is king. *It doesn't get much better that that!*

Horses during early morning workouts at Saratoga August 2016

The Whole Ball of Wax

For the most part, and at this time, I am rolling everything up into a big ball of wax. In most books, an outline would be laid out prior to telling the individual stories, but I have chosen to do this last. There is a method to my madness, and that is after writing so many stories—some lengthy and some somewhat shorter and more concise and an occasional snippet—I am going over these stories and rolling up the ball of wax. Should I attempt to peel back the layers like an onion at a later date and expand on some stories, or obviously add to another attempt in the future and follow up on this book, I could do so, especially if I have forgotten some stories. After all, looking back, I realize I'm speaking of drawing from memory close to sixty years and encompassing seven decades. You can now see how, reaching back in time, I have probably missed a fleeting moment that I can capture among the plethora of stories that are virtually endless.

Looking back to the mid-twentieth century, when the NYRA was known as the GNYA (or Greater New York Association), which included the now defunct Jamaica Racetrack, Aqueduct, Belmont, and Saratoga, my first experience with my buddy Jim. That's when we snuck into Aqueduct Racetrack and he put two dollars to win on *Daring Heart*, and this cheap claimer hit the wire in front, paying about $214 and change, hooking us forever. Easy money. Jim and I go back some seven decades, our wives only five decades, ha, a mere bag of shells some forty or fifty years. So I'll guide you down this road, occasionally stopping through the years over many miles and venues for a quick peek at some interesting narratives and anecdotes. I just recently reminded my friend Jim, who many years ago lived right off Sutter Avenue. Aqueduct's rear entrance to the clubhouse was at the end of Sutter Avenue. He had completely forgotten. I, for the most part, but for the pure goodness of my heart, I'll include him in saying that we've seen many incredible feats on and off the racetrack concerning Thoroughbreds. Oddly enough, I'll throw in a quick harness story or two in this work. Early on, we were sports fanatics. We would try to do it all with an insatiable desire not to allow any water to run under the bridge.

I can remember the late fifties and the early sixties as if it were yesterday. At one time, while only having weekends available since we did work, we would get together, hustle on down to Aqueduct on Saturday mornings, pick up the tele and the program, which were fifty cents and a quarter, do our numbers, and spend the whole day gambling on the ponies. Truly, it was a gamble, for what we knew could barely fill a thimble. We would look for certain situations such as blinkers on or off, change in riders, trainers, owners, distances six furlongs to a mile, to a mile and a quarter, dirt to grass, grass to dirt, and of course, bar shoe on or off and aluminum pad on or off. Along with our great handicapping abilities, the last two bar shoe or aluminum pad withstanding, we would bet a horse thinking that a bar shoe or aluminum pad on was something good, not derogatory. We were young and foolish know-it-alls, never bothering to check out what they were, always thinking any change was a positive. We couldn't understand why we lost more often than won.

I'll take a wild guess and say we finally figured it out in 1963, yippee! By the way, 1963 was the 100th anniversary of Saratoga, the year *Chateaugay* won the Derby, defeating *Never Bend, Candy Spots*, and *No Robbery*—all four were unbeaten till that point. The following year, 1964, was extremely interesting. The Triple Crown events started with the Kentucky Derby and drew a field including EP Taylor's Winfield Farms Canadian-bred, *Northern Dancer*, trained by Horatio Luro and ridden by the incomparable Bill Hartack. Understand that Bill Hartack and Eddie Arcaro were the only two jockeys ever to have won five Kentucky Derbies, followed by Willie Shoemaker with four. The difference between Arcaro and Hartack was simply that it took Arcaro twenty-one trips to the Derby to accomplish his feat, Bill Hartack ran in only twelve Kentucky Derbies, incredible, virtually without splitting hairs a 42% winning percentage. In my estimation, that will never be achieved again now or forever. *Northern Dancer* won the Derby, went on to win the second leg of the Triple Crown, the Preakness, and went on to the Belmont and lost his attempt at the Triple Crown to *Quadrangle* and *Roman Brother*, running third. Why didn't he become the first Triple Crown winner since *Citation* some sixteen years prior? In my humble opinion, very few people realize that Belmont was closed after the 1963 season for refurbishing. I know this for a fact, since my father worked construction and delivered the loam cushion by tractor trailer every day for months during that spring season, necessitating the Belmont to be run at Aqueduct, the one and only time. Belmont being a 1 $\frac{1}{2}$ mile oval, horses negotiated two turns. Aqueduct being a 1 $\frac{1}{8}$ mile oval, the start of the Belmont that year was near the top of the turn for home at the 3/8 pole, virtually making this race a three-turn race. I can't ever remember then or now seeing any three-year-old winning a 1 $\frac{1}{2}$ mile three-turn event, and if I'm wrong, I'll eat my hat. Connecting all the dots concerning the great *Northern Dancer,* he could possibly be the greatest equine specimen of all time, lest *Pegasus.* I'll explain why. Should he had run in 1964 at Belmont around two turns and won, he would have been a Triple Crown winner.

Now let's go to the breeding shed. I am sure most people will agree with me that *Northern Dancer* was more than likely the greatest sire of turf horses. Should you disagree, please find a way to let me know.

During the early sixties, I can mention such notables as Robert Fuller's *Fuller Brush,* owner of *Dancer's Image,* his subsequent disqualification in the Derby, mind you once and only, denying Bobby Ussery a Derby winner. Along with this honorable mention, I can speak of H. Allen Jerkens, the giant killer running a horse by the name of *California Girl,* high-priced claimer allowance horse in New York on Saturday and wheeling her back at Monmouth on Monday and winning that race. Winning two races with the same horse within three days was an incredible feat. Frankly, it may have been consecutive days if there was racing on Sundays in those years. Come to think of it, I have to call and mention this to Jimmy Jerkens.

Jimmy and I had a friend, Billy Verga, whose father owned horses and raced at Aqueduct and Belmont. I remember Billy saying that when I'm in the paddock area with my father next time, if I heard the horse was going to run, I'd tip my hat so he could see whether or not to play the horse in the race. Race day, and Verga had a horse running. Billy tipped his hat after listening to his father and trainer Bill Corbellini.

We bet the race and the horse won. A few weeks later, they had another horse running by the name of *Duby Cat*. I spoke to Billy, and he said, "The horse looks like he can win." It was in the 1960s. I was working on a construction project of the Nassau/Queens expressway right across from Aqueduct Racetrack. It was the fall and it was a Tuesday. *Duby Cat* was entered in the ninth race. All our friends at the Pavillon Bowl were told about this tip coming. Everybody kicked in money on Monday. I gathered a little less than $200 for everybody, including myself. The ninth race usually went off at 6:00 p.m. I was off and I was driving the big truck on the construction job. It was 4:00 p.m., two hours till race time. Rather than going to the track across the Belt Parkway, waiting two hours till race time, and possibly losing some money in an earlier race, I decided to return the truck to its home base at Savoy Avenue off Hempstead Turnpike across from Belmont Racetrack. It was a fifteen-minute drive to Belmont. I would park the truck, pick up my car, gas up, and drive fifteen, twenty minutes back to Aqueduct and get back twenty minutes to post time for the race. Best laid plans, yeah, fortunately, I stopped to gas up at Hempstead Turnpike and Wellington Avenue at the gas station owned by Gil Molkenten, one of the guys who bet the horse through me. He said, "What the hell are you doing here? You're supposed to be at the track putting the bet in."

I said, "Don't worry, we have plenty of time."

He said, "What are you talking about? It's the fall meet. They set the clocks back an hour on Saturday. The race is going off at 5:00 p.m., not 6:00 p.m. It's twenty to five right now. You'll never make it."

I said, "Oh damn," and took off like a rocket, got to the track, and went in the back way. While I was running to get on line to place the bet, I had bets win, place, and show. I had all sorts of bets, about $175 in bets, with two minutes to post, running to get on line. I headed straight for the $100 win window, figuring I'll just put $200 to win and cross my fingers the horse wins and I'll settle everything later. Literally one person in line in front of me and no minutes to post, he finished, and before I could get a word out, the bell rang and I knew the race was off. Instantly, I knew it was the kiss of death. He was the no. 12 horse going a $1^{1}/_{8}$ mile at Aqueduct, the worst place to be on the far outside going into the first turn, virtually an impossible position. I saw him get off dead last. I looked up at the board. I saw the no. 12 horse 13-1 being outrun. I quickly relaxed and said to myself, "Thank God. I saved a bundle." Figuring everybody would be happy that they didn't lose any money, *Duby Cat* still sat last, but he moved up slightly into the final turn, started to pick up horses one by one, came down the stretch still sitting eighth or ninth at the eighth pole, sixty feet off the rail, eight wide gets up to win a four horse three-minute photo, paying twenty-eight dollars and change.

Now I had the unenviable task of delivering the bad news that Tuesday evening. Saved by the pure grace of God by my friend Gil Molkenten, standing up and attesting to the fact that he knew I would never get the bet in, albeit I gallantly tried. From that, I learned a valuable lesson. Never take a bet from someone, for you shall be considered the bookie. Frankly, I should have delivered between $2,000 and $3,000 that evening, and everyone was drinking at the bar just before me and Gil had come in, otherwise, I may have been tarred, feathered, and run out of town on a rail.

Jimmy and I, for as long as I can remember, always had the angle on just about any kind of racing, or for that matter, gambling bet available. We both unilaterally thought if we could minimize the risk in the wager, we'd be far ahead of the curve. By the way, this is the one and only time I will refer to harness racing in this or any book in which I attach my name. Every once in a while, somebody would approach and start speaking of harness horses, thinking a horse is a horse of course, *au contraire*. When this happens, I quickly say, "No, I mean real horses." But in fact, Jimmy and I took virtually three months charting the half-mile ovals at both Yonkers and Roosevelt Raceway in the early seventies, maintaining a definite advantage to being on the rail. This is a fact. Let me tell you how it worked and work it did. On any given race evening, the no. 1 horse would win 1.53 races on every nine race card. That being a fact, we would wait till the no. 1 horse found a way to lose nine races on the entire card, then on two consecutive days following nine consecutive losses, making eighteen losing races from the one post, making two consecutive days zero for eighteen. This rarely happened when you do the math two consecutive days without a no. 1 horse winning. The track owed the investor 1.53 wins for each goose egg day times two, meaning that on that next card, the law of averages said there should be 4.59 winners from the one post. As the math indicated, over 50 percent are winners on the entire card, four or possibly five winners on that following day. This opportunity rarely came up, and when it did, it was fairly simple if you followed the numbers ten to win on the one in the first, followed by twenty to win on the no. 1 horse in the second, thirty to win on the no.1 horse in the third, forty to win in the fourth, fifty in the fifth, sixty in the sixth, seventy in the seventh, eighty in the eighth, and ninety in the ninth. This was a $450 total investment, quite a bit of cash in the early seventies. We placed the bet, and since there were no TVs or radios in those days, it was an advanced wager. We did it by late afternoon, ready to reap our rewards. After all that work, time, and money, we were rewarded, albeit three winners, not four or five. But still, the system worked. Unwittingly, we won the first race. Yahoo, ten to win at $4.20. Yahoo, again, we won the second race twenty to win at $3.80. We lost the third, coming real close, losing a photo with a 9–1 shot. Drats, but we did came back and won the fourth race, forty dollars to win at eight dollars even. We won three out of the first four races, returning twenty-one dollars, then thirty-eight dollars, and then $160, equaling $219. With five races to go, only down $231, with the big bets coming up, we felt we were home free. Much to our regret, we ran second three times in three photos in the next five races, two out of the three at big balloons, 12–1 and 19–1 along with the third one at 3–1. We coulda, shoulda, woulda walked away with a few grand, never again to have the persistence, time, and effort. It was long and tedious to try again.

Looking back, we often spoke of three out of nine 33 1/3 winning percentage. Truth be told, we would rather have won the seventh, eighth, and ninth races rather than the first, second, and fourth. We were good, but I'd certainly rather be lucky than good. Not another sulky driver or half-mile track to be spoken of again.

It seems to me that I have exhausted this complete school of thought, expanding from the fifties through the present day, not only with owners, trainers, jockeys, great Thoroughbreds over an enormous time span dating back to the fifties with *Bold Ruler* up through the seventies with the incredible *Secretariat, Ruffian, Seattle Slew, Affirmed,* and even through the more recent *American Pharaoh.* This compilation of short stories is just the tip of the iceberg. Truth be told, I could go on forever with hundreds or possibly thousands of other stories that will not only whet your appetite but engulf you and mesmerize you for hours and hours on end.

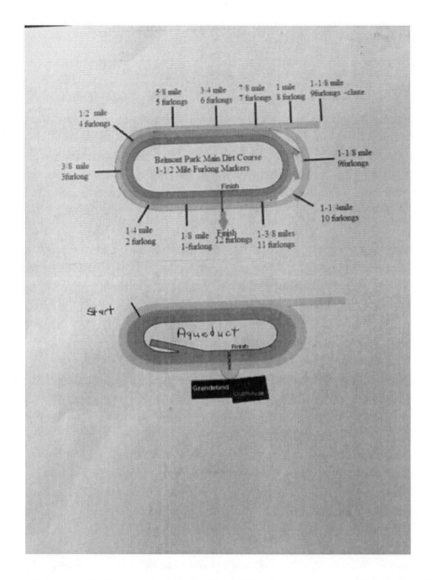

Belmont Stakes raced at Belmont Park every year except 1964 when being renovated. Top caption race run once around the track start to finish, two turns., 1 ½ miles. Lower caption 1964 race run at Aqueduct 1 1/8 mile track, necessitating start as indicated same 1 ½ mile Belmont stakes run around three turns. In my opinion Triple Crown compromised by additional third turn.

Acknowledgements

We would like to thank the many people that we have leaned on for support, information and assistance through the years in putting this project together. It has metamorphasized and come to fruition through hard work and dedication.

We would like to thank our family for putting up with our antics and encouraging us to go on and especially our grandchildren who are forever asking questions about when the book will be completed.

Thanks also to our close friends Jim Dundon and Jerry Sifert who have patiently put up with us during this process.

We would like to thank our new friends Jonathan Smart, Jonathan Sheppard, Mike Sassin, Danny Wright and Marshall Cassidy for all the time and help afforded us despite their busy schedules, and also Betsy and Cathy at the Keeneland Library for all their archival work. Special thanks to our friend Todd Robertson for his graphic artwork in creating the cover for Pony Tales and Mike Valentino for his editing of the original manuscript.

Thanks to our publisher Xlibris for affording us this opportunity and special thanks to Xena our Sr. Publishing Consultant and Iris our submissions representative, with their expertise and business like but bubbly attitudes, it has been a pleasure working with them.

To any of those who have been with us over the course of the years and whose names we have failed to mention we sincerely thank you.

Edwards Brothers Malloy
Thorofare, NJ USA
December 9, 2016